W9-CFO-252

SAINTS & POLITICIANS

AFRICAN STUDIES SERIES

EDITORIAL BOARD
John Dunn, *Lecturer in Political Science and Fellow of King's College, Cambridge*
Jack Goody, *Professor of Social Anthropology and Fellow of St John's College, Cambridge*
J.M. Lonsdale, *Assistant Lecturer in History and Fellow of Trinity College, Cambridge*
A.F. Robertson, *Director of the African Studies Centre and Fellow of Darwin College, Cambridge*

The African Studies Series is a collection of monographs and general studies which reflect the interdisciplinary interests of the African Studies Centre at Cambridge. Volumes to date have combined historical, anthropological, economic, political and other perspectives. Each contribution has assumed that such broad approaches can contribute much to our understanding of Africa, and that this may in turn be of advantage to specific disciplines.

BOOKS IN THIS SERIES

1 *City Politics: A Study of Léopoldville, 1962–3* – J. S. LA FONTAINE
2 *Studies in Rural Capitalism in West Africa* – POLLY HILL
3 *Land Policy in Buganda* – HENRY W. WEST
4 *The Nigerian Military: A Sociological Analysis of Authority and Revolt, 1960–7* – ROBIN LUCKHAM
5 *The Ghanaian Factory Worker: Industrial Man in Africa* – MARGARET PEIL
6 *Labour in the South African Gold Mines, 1911–69* – FRANCIS WILSON
7 *The Price of Liberty: Personality and Politics in Colonial Nigeria* – KENNETH W. J. POST and GEORGE D. JENKINS
8 *Subsistence to Commercial Farming in Present Day Buganda: An Economic and Anthropological Survey* – AUDREY I. RICHARDS, FORD STURROCK and JEAN M. FORTT (eds.)
9 *Dependence and Opportunity: Political Change in Ahafo* – JOHN DUNN and A. F. ROBERTSON
10 *African Railwaymen: Solidarity and Opposition in an East African Labour Force* – R. D. GRILLO
11 *Islam and Tribal Art in West Africa* – RENÉ A. BRAVMANN
12 *Modern and Traditional Elites in the Politics of Lagos* – P. D. COLE
13 *Asante in the Nineteenth Century: The Structure and Evolution of a Political Order* – IVOR WILKS
14 *Culture, Tradition and Society in the West African Novel* – E. N. OBIECHINA
15 *Saints and Politicians: Essays in the Organisation of a Senegalese Peasant Society* – DONAL B. CRUISE O'BRIEN

SAINTS & POLITICIANS

Essays in the organisation of a Senegalese peasant society

Donal B. Cruise O'Brien

Lecturer in the School of Oriental and African Studies, University of London

CAMBRIDGE UNIVERSITY PRESS

SOC
DT
549.42
C77

Published by the Syndics of the Cambridge University Press
Bentley House, 200 Euston Road, London NW1 2DB
American Branch: 32 East 57th Street, New York, N.Y. 10022

© Cambridge University Press 1975

Library of Congress Catalogue Card Number: 74–82221

ISBN: 0 521 20572 7

First published 1975

Photoset and printed
in Great Britain by
REDWOOD BURN LIMITED
Trowbridge & Esher

Robert Manning Strozier Library

JUN 24 1975

Tallahassee, Florida

CONTENTS

PREFACE AND ACKNOWLEDGMENTS

The groundwork for these essays lies in research conducted in the Wolof zone of Senegal in 1966–7; some two hundred formal interviews, numerous other discussions and conversations which were supplemented by library and archival research in Dakar and Paris. Due reference is made below to written sources, which may be available for consultation (and verification) by others. Oral sources, on the other hand, are named only in a very few exceptional instances (Thierno Sow, Cheikh Kane, Momar Sakho, Sérigne Mbacké Nioro). This is not of course to deprecate the very great contribution of other Senegalese informants, but there seems little point here in referring the reader to individuals whom he may be most unlikely ever to meet (any concerned researcher need only request the necessary details).

Some of the results of this field research have already been published in book form (*The Mourides of Senegal*, Oxford: Clarendon Press, 1971), these essays being a substantial development and extension of that presentation. The essays are intended both to be more systematically interpretive of research findings already published and to cover a much wider area of concern.

Apart from the great debt which I owe to many Senegalese friends and informants, I should here acknowledge the help of those scholars (concerned with themes related to these essays) who have helped both in discussions and often in allowing me to see pre-publication drafts of their work

(Samin Amin, Jonathan Barker, Jean Copans, Martin Klein, among others). Valuable critical comments and suggestions have also been made, in various seminar discussions of drafts of these essays, by many colleagues – Ernest Gellner and M. G. Smith perhaps in particular. My thanks are due to Jack Goody, at whose original suggestion this collection of essays was written and compiled. Acknowledgment is also of course due to those who have separately published drafts or sections of some of these essays (in French or in English).* Without prejudice to other friends and colleagues, I must finally recognise that my greatest scholarly debt has been to my wife Rita – an expert, patient and most gentle critic.

January 1974 D.C.O.B.

* 'Cooperators and Bureaucrats: Class Formation in a Senegalese Peasant Society', in *Africa*, Vol. XLI, No. 4, 1971, is extensively revised and adapted in Chapter 4 below. 'Chefs, Saints, et Bureaucrates', in A. Abdel-Malek (ed.), *Sociologie de L'Impérialisme*, Paris, Eds. Anthropos, 1971, is revised and much expanded in Chapter 3 below. 'Don Divin, Don Terrestre' is slightly revised (and translated) in Chapter 2, from *Archives Européennes de Sociologie*, Vol. XV, No. 1, 1974.

Introduction

As these lines are written, people are dying of hunger and hunger's attendant diseases in the Wolof region of Senegal (as indeed they are dying, often in much greater numbers, throughout the West African Sahel). Wolof fatalities, as yet, are few in number – above all the old, the weak, and the very young. The great majority will at least survive this hungry season (1973) to reap the next harvest. Few however, in rural areas, can face the long-term ecological future with any degree of confidence.

The Wolof farm in the savannah region of north-western Senegal, the Senegal and Gambia rivers to north and south, the Atlantic ocean to the west and the Ferlo desert to the east. No part of this region could be described as agriculturally fertile, soils being (in varying degrees) poor in humus, dry and sandy. And as soil deteriorates with over-cultivation, so the desert still expands from the north and east. Agricultural techniques have improved only very slowly with French technical guidance, productivity per acre remaining low despite the limited use of chemical fertilisers and some light machinery.[1] Wolof response to the pressure of rising population, and of rising expectations for at least some imported 'luxuries', in these circumstances has been to extend the area under cultivation. This means a neglect of necessary fallow periods even on relatively good soils, and new agricultural settlement in ever poorer soils. In present conditions, it can only mean the further encroachment of the desert. This grim logic has long been apparent to the trained agronomist, but even to the layman it is strikingly enough illustrated towards the end of any dry season. The savannah then takes on the appearance of a semi-desert expanse, a few trees and hardy shrubs dotted through the dead grass, strong winds driving the sand across the landscape. In some areas true desert dunes are already in the process of formation.[2]

To report that the Wolof are living in the shadow of death, although certainly very necessary, is equally certainly quite inadequate to understand how they continue to live at all: even, disturbing as this too may seem, to live rather better than most of their neighbours. To gain any real understanding of their present predicament, one must first understand Wolof history – the processes (at least since French conquest) which have led to the present situation. The outlines of this situation, as reported by the journalist or representative of an international relief organisation, may seem simple enough – too many people trying to live on too little land. And put in these terms, the problem *is* indeed simple – although, alas, no 'solution' of equal simplicity is readily to hand. But there is obviously much more to the Wolof than the stark evidence of today's rural starvation: the purpose of these essays then is both to present a historical analysis of changes brought about (in large part) by colonial rule and to suggest an interpretation of the present situation which does some justice to its real complexity.

Good ethnographic evidence, studies of at least some Wolof villages by trained social anthropologists, could be of great assistance in an enquiry of this kind. And it may seem surprising, given the simple fact that the Wolof account for one third of Senegal's population, that no such study exists. English and American anthropologists have indeed worked among the Wolof of neighbouring Gambia,[3] but their findings although helpful cannot be assumed to hold for the Senegalese Wolof – if only because the latter have undergone a quite different colonial experience. Many monographs have on the other hand been written (though very few published) on Senegalese Wolof villages, of widely varying thoroughness but in any case not showing much evidence of basic ethnographic training on the part of any of their authors (some of them administrators, colonial or post-colonial, recently some geographers and some economists).[4] One Senegalese social anthropologist (Abdoulaye Diop) is presently engaged on a full-length study of Wolof social organisation, the results of which may go far to fill the gap, but for the present one must acknowledge the simple non-existence of much basic data, above all on the detail of kinship patterns at a local level.

These essays themselves are not designed to fill that gap, although some evidence for at least one segment of Wolof society is indicated (above all, in 'Land, cash, and charisma', below). This author's fieldwork among the rural Wolof, in 1966–7, provided only partial evidence on kinship structures, which here is completed so far as possible by a selective use of material (copious enough, at least) from other sources. Certain very broad generalisations can on this basis be made safely enough – in particular that the partially matrilineal character of pre-colonial Wolof society has almost wholly given way to the patrilineal forms dictated by Islam. It may also (perhaps less safely) be asserted that in the Wolof case social and political structure can be fully understood only by methods which go beyond the traditional approaches of social anthropology. In discussing the Wolof now, one is necessarily involved in an understanding both of a commercial market and a state structure which include the whole territory of Senegal. For historical reasons, the most important of which deserve some preliminary mention, the Wolof have long ceased to be (if indeed they ever were) a discrete tribal entity, a social group with clearly defined boundaries – whether cultural or other.

Culture contact, first, has had its effect both on internal Wolof organisation and (almost by definition) on the relations of the Wolof to their neighbours. Islam is the first notable cultural influence to mention, first both in overall importance and in simple chronological order. Wolof contacts with Muslims to the north and east date back at least to the eleventh century, and the long, slow, and fluctuating process of Islamisation can be traced from that time. Whatever the stresses and contradictions inherent in that process (for some of which, see 'Warlord, saint, and knight' below), it was certainly very firmly established by the mid nineteenth century and it is now apparently quite complete. Today, to be Wolof is necessarily to be Muslim. Pre-Islamic Wolof culture, insofar as it is ascertainable at all, is ascertainable only through the accounts of earlier European travellers and through a few vestigial beliefs and practices which still survive. Even these latter remnants are now overladen with Sufi Islam, a culture ultimately dictated by Arabic texts although necessarily mediated by the learned among local holy men. A blurring of tribal boundaries is a logical outcome of Islamisation, as the Wolof's immediate neighbours are also Muslims. This 'blurring' is also facilitated by a compatibility of social structures between the Wolof and each of their principal neighbours – stratification of society in very similar (almost indeed identical) hierarchies of class and caste. One may now much more readily intermarry at the same social rank, between tribes, than within the tribe but between ranks.

The second significant dimension of culture contact has been that implicit in Wolof relations with the French, established on the coast as traders from the seventeenth century, as an increasingly effective colonial government from the mid nineteenth century, as a hegemonic power in Senegal to this day. French cultural penetration has always applied principally if not exclusively to the towns, where French-language education has been concentrated, but it is an important hazard of colonial fate that Senegal's principal towns (Dakar, St Louis, Thiès, Kaolack) are all located either on Wolof territory proper or in areas readily accessible to Wolof migration and (in local terms) eventual dominance. The sub-elite of colonial intermediaries, and the Senegalese governing elite today (of whatever tribal origin) have written in French and spoken in Wolof. From this elite there has certainly been some process of cultural diffusion (most happily perhaps in gastronomic terms) from France even to the rural and illiterate Wolof majority.

Where France is concerned, nonetheless, it would of course be distortive to see 'influence' primarily as cultural. This particular culture contact was only part of a more important relation, the real language of which was that of power and money. Seen in these broader terms, the colonial impact on the Wolof has been enormous, uniquely so among Senegalese peoples. Other tribes may have yielded more to the French in cultural terms, notably the 'pagan' tribes chosen for intensive Catholic missionary activity (the Diola and Serer). But the Wolof, while immune to such proselytisation (as Muslims), also became almost inextricably involved in new institutional structures introduced and dominated by the French – those of the market economy and of the semi-bureaucratic colonial state.

The Wolof certainly have derived real material benefits, gains relative both to other Senegalese communities and even to their own pre-colonial situation, from the operation of these colonial structures. They have also been faced by new sorts of problems, some less obviously resoluble than others.

No simple cost-benefit arithmetic can be applied to the gains and losses occasioned by colonial rule, especially since the colonial mechanisms are still at work today with no final outcome in sight. But it may be worth remark that the colonial relation now seems to have been most damaging for Wolof society less in the frequently-condemned evils of economic exploitation and political subjugation than in colonial rule's apparently most unequivocal benefits. The suppression of internal war in the Senegal area, the containment of epidemic disease, improved infant care, relief food supplies for famine periods, all contributed to the rapid growth of Wolof (and other Senegalese) population. The expansion of a new cash crop economy made possible a short-term enrichment of this population, but over the past ten years or more it has become apparent that agricultural production can no longer meet the basic needs of ever-increasing numbers. And if production still stagnates, population still grows. Demographic statistics in Senegal are only approximations, but (even allowing a very wide margin of error) the trend is clear enough: some 460,000 Wolof at the time of the first world war, some 650,000 for the second world war (statistics in each case compiled with military recruitment in mind), and in 1960–1, 1,103,000 (the most reliable population estimate ever made in Senegal, based on a demographers' sample of 10% of the total population). Demographers now estimate continuing population growth at between 2.5% and 2.7% per year.[5] And it may be noted, with due reservation as to the reliability of these statistics, that there is no indication of more rapid increases among the Wolof than among other Senegalese peoples – consistently over time, the Wolof are held to account for some one third of Senegal's total population, by far the largest single tribe. The important conclusion from this evidence is that population growth does not appear to have been especially favoured by the Wolof's relatively high exposure to urbanisation and to commercial agriculture. The destructive impact of population growth, the often acute stresses on social solidarity where resources become ever scarcer in relation to numbers competing, cannot in particular be blamed on the peanut.

The peanut nonetheless in other terms has had enormous effects, both destructive and reconstructive, on Wolof society. This apparently innocuous plant seems to have been introduced to the Senegal area as far back as the sixteenth century, brought from South America by Portuguese slave-traders for local use as a food crop. The French in the early nineteenth century grew it experimentally as one among several possible future export crops: no firm conclusions were drawn from these trials (notably by Governor Roger, in 1824). But by 1847, having recognised the limited agricultural possibilities of most of Senegal's sandy soils, Governor Protêt (prophetically at least in his own terms) announced that 'peanuts will save the country'.[6] And 'save the country', or at least provide for a viable colonial economy, they went on to do: peanuts have for almost a century accounted for the great bulk (up to 90%) of Senegal's export value, with the Wolof growing the bulk (over 60%) of the crop. The increase of annual exports was very rapid in the early colonial period, as the following statistics for territorial export tonnages show: 1875, 13.9 tons; 1885, 45.1 tons; 1895, 51.6; 1905, 96.2; 1915, 303.1; 1925, 453.7; 1936, 487.3; 1948, 451.0; 1958, 808.0.[7] (After the second world war came a new spurt in output: detailed annual statistics for the period since independence in 'Bureaucrats and Cooperators', below.)

What these figures have meant to the Wolof is that they have become a people of peanut peasants. Low profit margins, and low economies of scale, effectively precluded white settlement in rural Senegal. There are still no major Wolof landowners, although there are some large land holdings – without legal title, and with an informal title which has to date always proved conditional and insecure.

Family plots of no more than a few acres (10–20 in most cases) are at present the established norm. These peasant farms do retain a certain viability, independent of the market economy, in the cultivation of millet for subsistence. But they have also become dangerously dependent on the peanut, which is grown largely (though not exclusively) for sale. The 'dangerous dependence' on the peanut, which means that peasants may starve when the rains fail, also applies to the Senegalese state. The peanut was the quickest and simplest way to make the colony pay, and the same logic continues to apply in Senegal since national independence. Without the peanut harvest, no other local resources make it possible simply to pay for the state apparatus – which in turn, means above all to pay the salaries of state employees. So government policy, while frequently recognising a need for agricultural and other economic 'diversification', has in fact consistently been to encourage the monoculture which official speeches condemn. Wolof peasants, who know very well that the peanut until now has allowed them a (marginally) higher living standard than most of their neighbours, have been willing to take the risks involved – locally seen, and quite correctly so, as 'a gamble'. Albeit a gamble in which the stakes are getting uncomfortably high.

The colonial state introduced the peanut as an export crop, and supervised the rapid extension of its cultivation, while the post-colonial version of the same state apparatus has brought the internal marketing of the crop ever more securely within its own control (while French oil manufacturers continue to control the marketing process beyond the boundaries of Senegal). For the Wolof, state dominance and state profits are necessarily seen in somewhat ambiguous terms: from one angle, 'the state' seems unambiguously to have economic interests in direct conflict with 'the peasants'. But from another angle, if one considers that the interests of 'the state' represent little more than the aggregated interests of state employees (and by extension of their dependents), the matter becomes more complex. Wolof peasants largely provide for the state apparatus in economic terms, but Wolof officials also dominate the state in political terms. And if this suggests possibilities of some local variant of class conflict within Wolof society, it must be recalled that even the poorer rural Wolof feel a certain superiority over other Senegalese. The Wolof have not done so badly out of the colonial and post-colonial state, relative to Senegal's other tribes. They have a higher living standard, they get preferential treatment in the allocation of government finance (roads, rail, schools, the various forms of 'development' expenditure), and they have a certain shared pride both in these (often meagre) relative material privileges and in their communal political power (an argument developed in 'Clans, clienteles, and communities', below).

If these few remarks may have served to sketch a necessary background against which these essays may be understood, it remains to say a little more of the theme of the essays themselves. This theme is essentially a political one, that of the organisational response of the Wolof people to colonial rule – the response of particular individuals, of given categories of political actors, of segments within Wolof society and (to some extent) of the Wolof people as a whole. The argument running through the essays is that the French impact on Wolof society was effective enough in terms of the limited objectives of the colonial power, in dismantling most pre-colonial political institutions (states and chieftaincies) and in providing a rudimentary machinery for the maintenance of public order. But colonial authority, it is held, always lacked both the social legitimacy and the institutional solidity needed to have a firm control of political life among the Wolof. In this situation of governmental fragility, and in particular given the very rapid economic and social change produced by the generalisation of the market mechanism, there was always room for initiative among the subjects (see 'Chiefs, saints and bureaucrats', below). The same laws of institutional fragility, at least where the formal apparatus of state is concerned, continue to apply today. And this may be taken to imply what is the principal concern of these essays, the importance of the various intermediaries who stand between the nominally bureaucratic state (colonial or post-colonial) and the rural mass of Wolof subjects. Two very broad categories may be applied to these intermediaries, the categories indicated by the title of this collection. Let us then briefly outline a description of the heterogeneous reality indicated by each of the labels, 'saint' and 'politician'.

'Saint' is the single most appropriate English-language designation for leaders of the three Sufi Muslim orders (*tariqas*) which between them claim the spiritual allegiance of the entire rural Wolof population – the Tijaniyya (roughly 60% of the Wolof total), the Qadiriyya (10%) and the Mouride (30%).[8] Each of these orders has its own, Arabic, nomenclature for such holy men (*shaikh*, *muqaddam*, etc.), but the overall label saint applies to those who are considered to be the bearers of a (now quasi-hereditary) charisma – or in Sufi terminology, *baraka*. The term *baraka* implies a special spiritual grace, a special position with God which may include the power to redeem souls. But it also, in wordly life, has come to imply political as well as economic power, in other terms a special position with the authorities of the state. The power of the saint, spiritually sanctioned, is truly a legitimate authority. And the bureaucratic state, originally imposed by the French, has remained chronically deficient in moral sanctions of any kind. The state authorities, to work effectively among the Wolof, have thus been irrevocably compelled to come to terms with the Sufi saints. And the saints, fully conscious of the strength of their position, have learned how to drive a hard bargain. The state must provide material rewards to win their compliance, and the saints of course can then reinforce authority over their own disciples by passing on a share of these rewards. Crucially perhaps, these saints are the richest and most powerful people to have chosen to remain residents of the rural Wolof zone. The saints as yet in great majority seem unattracted by the relative luxuries of Dakar, powerful magnet for all other Wolof ambition. Like machine politicians in at least this respect, the saints appear to prefer power to luxury, and they choose to remain where their power lies – in the villages.

The single label, 'politician', the manipulator of power over others, must obviously cover a very wide range of empirical possibilities. In this case-study, with its primary focus on intermediary relationships between the state and rural society, a few of the most significant typical roles may be distinguished. The first is already suggested, and remains a recurring theme below, the saint *as* politician. The second is the chief, either the semi-despotic ruler of the pre-colonial Wolof states or the (differently, semi-despotic) colonial appointee with a thin claim to 'customary' authority. Chiefs enjoyed little popularity even before French conquest, and under colonial rule, they lost first their independence and then the coercive basis of their control over subjects. If the French, against their originally firm desire, were driven back to a policy of 'indirect' rule, this did not help the Wolof chiefs. The third typical intermediary role is that of the Wolof bureaucrat, whose loyalty at least in principle is to his hierarchial superior: this ladder of hierarchy leads directly to the towns, at first to the French and later to the French-educated African elite. Such norms of hierarchy, and of specified official jurisdiction, laid down a clear responsibility to perform certain basic tasks on the state's behalf – to encourage commercial agriculture, to raise taxes, and to maintain public order. Official norms however have tended to obscure or disguise the truly political nature of the bureaucrat's role, the scope effectively allowed for discretionary action, the manipulation of personal relationships, the selective exercise of power. The fourth characteristic intermediary role (not given much detailed attention in these essays) is again one which is not explicitly or always very obviously a political one, that of the trader. In Senegal at least, however, money cannot be made in large amounts without effective access to political power. Whether dealing with government-allocated import licences, or (often illicitly) in money-lending and the marketing of export produce, the trader must have his friends in high political office. Wolof traders, insofar as they have improved their competitive position within an internal market system originally dominated by the French and (at a lower level) the Lebanese, have done so by successful manipulation of political alliances.

The fifth, final, most obviously and explicitly 'political' of intermediary roles is that of the elected candidates of the principal Senegalese political parties. Such parties, at least with African comparisons in mind, are a peculiarly venerable Senegalese institution, going back at least to the time of the first world war. In the period until 1945, these parties were nominally restricted in their activity to those few coastal towns with the franchise, but in practice even in the early period party politicians cultivated certain connections in rural Wolof society. Since the second world war, and with the emergence of the dominant and then single party system of the *Union Progressiste Sénégalaise*, party notables have steadily increased the patronage resources under their control – which are allocated in return for votes, more diffuse expressions of support and (sometimes) money.

The selection of these five role types may be taken as no more than a necessary introductory simplification. Any one category is obviously subject to considerable internal differentiation, notably to some gradation of wealth and power which exercise of the role allows any individual to accumulate. Roles also are less clearly distinguishable than the above categorisation may suggest. In the extreme case, one individual might (perhaps for distinct occasions) be saint, chief, bureaucrat, trader, *and* party politician. In almost all empirical instances, the individual who may be given one of these labels in effect fills more than one of the roles.

More significant than these rather obvious, even self-evident preliminary reservations, is the positive argument (emerging most explicitly in the last of these essays) for the existence of a characteristic network of linkages between such political roles. Bureaucratic state, political party, market economy, holy order, each 'sub-system' is fully intelligible for this analysis only within an overall pattern of alliances between individuals which cut across sub-system boundaries. The pattern which emerges from such alliances, locally termed that of 'clan politics', amounts in its own bizarre way to the structure of a Senegalese political system. This conclusion is reached without recourse to the dry abstractions of modern 'systems analysis', and without any assumption of a *necessary* binding coherence of political action. Empirical observation of Senegalese political life does here suggest that (beyond the evident individual strife for power) there is an underlying coherence in Senegalese politics. This pattern can be reconstructed with a proper understanding both of the mechanisms of shared material interest (patronage, graft) and of the 'ideal' dimensions of solidarity (communal and other loyalties). The material and ideal dimensions of politics of course overlap, and the pattern emerging may seem confusing enough to an outsider.

In its own terms, however, and certainly to local political participants, the logic of clan politics is clear enough. The presentation of that logic, in an outsider's terms, may be taken as the outcome of these five essays.

It may be useful to the reader, finally, to make an introductory mention of each of the five individual essays presented here, and to suggest the sequence which they are intended to provide. The first essay is a study of three outstanding Wolof personalities at the time of French conquest, viewed against the background of crisis in Wolof society at that time. The second deals with the legacy of this crisis and of these three individuals, organisationally expressed in the Mouride brotherhood. The third examines the important political dimensions in the real workings of the administrative structure which the French imposed upon the Wolof. The fourth analyses the peanut marketing network which the French also imposed, and which has changed the face of Wolof society, as it has worked both before and after Senegalese independence (1960). The fifth and final essay deals with electoral or party politics, 'clan politics', which must take account of the mechanisms described in the previous essays. Cumulatively therefore the essays are consistently political in focus, whether saintliness or cash transactions be the primary subject in a given instance. The subjects treated tend to move from the specific and particular (three heroic characters, one segment of Wolof society) to the more general and inclusive (the Wolof people as a whole, whose politics must necessarily be understood in relation to other, non-Wolof, peoples within the state of Senegal). The hegemonic position of the Wolof in Senegal implies that the 'inclusive' approach be an analysis of Senegalese politics as a whole: from the particularities of Wolof politics, the collection thus concludes with a structural outline of a sociology of the Senegalese state.

NOTES

1 Productivity per hectare has improved very little overall since the early years of this century, consistently falling short of the official objective of one metric ton of peanuts per hectare. In overall terms, the relatively good yields from newly-cultivated areas are offset by the trend to soil deterioration in established agricultural areas. For detailed statistics and an economist's analysis, République du Sénégal, Conseil Economique et Social, 'Note sur la Situation Agricole du Sénégal', Dakar 1966 (unpublished), Annexe 1. Also S. Amin, *L'Afrique de l'Ouest Bloquée*, Paris: Eds. de Minuit, 1971, pp. 23-64 (a useful chapter on the Senegalese peanut economy, drawing heavily on the work of A. Vanhaeverbeke of the University of Louvain).

2 A very full (939 pages) geographer's account of Senegal's ecological problems is given in P. Pélissier, *Les Paysans du Sénégal. Les Civilisations Agraires du Cayorà la Casamance*, St Yrieix: Imp. Fabrègue, 1966.

3 Published results in D. Gamble, *The Wolof of Senegambia*, London: International African Institute, 1957. Also a number of articles by D. W. Ames: 'Belief in "Witches" among the rural Wolof of the Gambia' in *Africa*, Vol. XXIX, No. 3, 1959; 'The Economic Base of Wolof Polygyny' in *South-Western Journal of Anthropology*, Vol. XI, No. 4, 1955; 'The Selection of Mates, Courtship and Marriage among the Wolof in *Bulletin de l'Institut Français d'Afrique Noire*, Vol. XVIII, Ser. B, Nos. 1–2, 956; 'Wolof Cooperative Work Groups' in W. R. Bascom and M. J. Herskovits, *Continuity and Change in African Cultures*, Chicago: University of Chicago Press, 1959.

4 Various administrators' studies of the colonial period are preserved in Paris at the *Centre de Hautes Etudes Administratives sur l'Afrique et l'Asie Modernes* and the *Ecole Nationale de la France d'Outre-Mer*. For the post-colonial period unpublished documentation is gathered in Dakar at the *Ecole Nationale D'Economie Appliquée* and the various governmental agencies associated with the *Ministère du Plan*. The best village case studies yet available are those published by J. Copans *et al.*, *Maintenance Social et Changement Economique au Sénégal*, Vol. I, Dakar, O.R.S.T.O.M., 1972.

5 Demographic statistics, historical and contemporary, may be gleaned from a wide variety of French and Senegalese official sources: these are collected and accurately re-stated in L. Verrière, 'La Population du Sénégal', Thèse de Doctorat, Faculté de Droit et Sciences Economiques, Université de Dakar, 1965.

6 Quoted in G. Hardy, *La Mise en Valeur du Sénégal de 1817 à 1854*, Paris: Larose, 1921, p. 289 (a very well documented source on the economic history of this early period).

7 Detailed figures for annual peanut harvests, showing a wide seasonal variation as well as longer-term fluctuations, in X. Guiraud, *L'Arachide*

Sénégalaise, Paris: Librairie Technique et Economique, 1937 (p. 37 and throughout). Also République du Sénégal, Conseil Economique et Social, *op. cit.* Annexe 1.

8 These 'percentages', frequently re-stated in a wide variety of sources, can be no more than very approximate estimates. The only reasonably precise figures on Wolof religious affiliations, which show Tijanis at 61% of the Wolof total, then Mourides (28–30%) and a lower proportion of Qadiris (6–7%) are those of urban censuses of Dakar and Thiès in the nineteen-fifties: Afrique Occidentale Française, Haut Commisariat, Service de la Statistique Générale, *Commune Mixte de Thiès: Recensement de 1953* (Dakar n.d.) and *Recensement Démographique de Dakar (1955)*, Paris, 1958.

1

WARLORD, SAINT AND KNIGHT

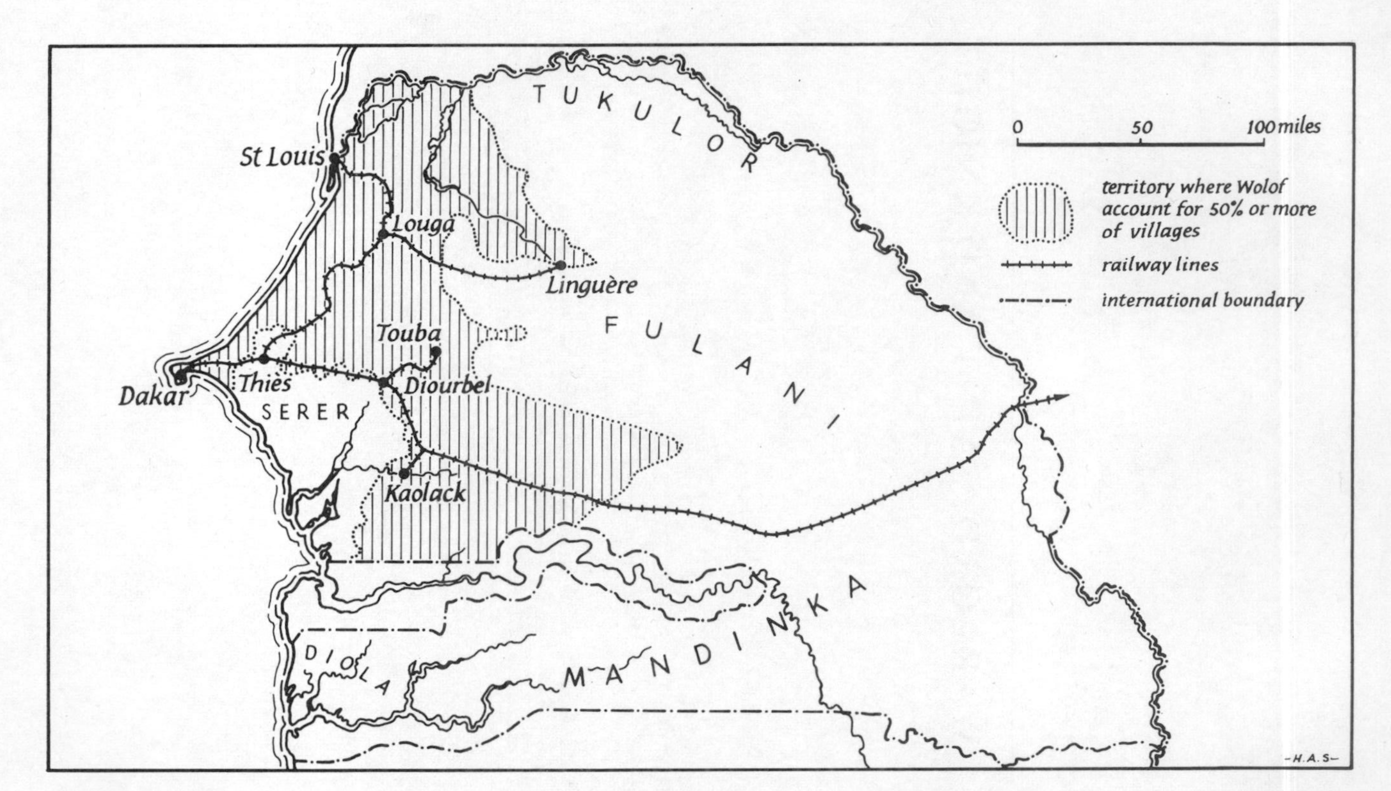

Wolof zone in Senegal, showing railways and principal towns and indicating other major tribal areas. Adapted from 'Cartes des Repartitions Ethniques de la Population', in Republique du Sénégal, *Plan Quadriennal de Développement*, 1961, 3d fig. ff. p. 2.

WARLORD, SAINT AND KNIGHT

Leading roles and supporting cast in a historical drama

The drama which provides the subject of this study is the social crisis surrounding the French conquest of the Wolof states, in the broadest terms a confrontation of indigenous social and political organisation with an alien imperialism. The immediate outcome of this critical confrontation, dealt with below ('Land, cash and charisma'), was a new form of indigenous organisation based on a surreptitiously revolutionary set of beliefs. The focus here is less on the broad social groups or categories involved, although these must certainly be outlined if the drama is to be intelligible, than on three individual personalities. These leading actors may each be regarded as exemplary of particular social groups and collective beliefs, and as representative of the aspirations of their followers. But each in his distinct style is also a leader of heroic stature, in a position to guide the particular direction in which social forces moved.

These three lives, studied separately and in relation to each other, may be taken to illustrate the argument that outstanding individuals may be in a position to direct social impulses in a manner which is not necessarily *dictated* to them – either, in this case, by the people whose aspirations they represented, or by the powerful external agency of the French conquerors. It may be accepted as a platitude in sociologically informed history that (in Marx's words) men do not make their own history 'just as they please',[1] but equally it must be recognised both in this case and indeed in general that men do make their own history. And some men more than others. Particular leaders, through force of character, through a particularly acute perception of new possibilities in a political situation, perhaps also through recognition of changing popular needs, may exert incalculable influence on a historical outcome. The scope for new individual initiatives must be unusually large in a period such as this, one of very rapid change in every aspect of social organisation. But the influence of these leaders on historical events, through their actions and in some cases inactions, is in any case undeniable. The outcome can only be inevitable after it has happened.

The three principal actors in this historical drama, the Warlord, the Saint and the Knight, make up a triangle of personal qualities. Each in his particular manner was perceived as altogether exceptional in his own time, if not always as hero at least as villain on the grand scale, and their importance is if anything further emphasised by the Wolof today. Their life-histories are closely intertwined both in historical reality, in so far as this can be precisely established now, and in the semi-mythological perceptions of the mass audience. This 'audience' again is by no means to be regarded as one of passive spectators. They also, in their own manner and to the extent of their powers, were engaged in 'making their own history'. They were in fact themselves on the stage, and one perceptive early observer of these events made the judgment that in this drama 'the chorus plays the leading role'.[2] Such a judgment is developed in this essay and the next, and is in many ways accepted, but it is also excessive in failing to recognise the full importance of the role of one principal actor. In the version of the drama presented here it is precisely this principal, the 'Knight', who is seen to have played the dominant part. Each of the three in any case has a close relation to the 'chorus', each may be seen to incarnate collective desires and to organise and articulate the aspirations of those who themselves were otherwise inarticulate and disorganised.

The chorus of the Wolof masses were at this time, at the end of the nineteenth century, victims of a generalised dislocation of their established way of life. Two powerful outside forces worked to dislocate Wolof society, both at a structural level (social, economic and political ties) and at the level of beliefs (cultural or ideological). Each of these outside agencies, French colonisers and militant Muslim puritans, had been long established in the Senegal area, effectively for more than a century in both cases, but each also became an increasingly potent force towards the conclusion of the nineteenth century. The crisis which they had generated came to a head in the year 1886, the date of the final decisive defeat by the French of the remnants of the Wolof armies. The same year saw the foundation, in the immediate aftermath of this battle, of a new Muslim brotherhood which recruited and organised those who had been most disoriented by this defeat. French conquest then made possible a reconciliation between two great factions of Wolof society, militant Muslims and 'backsliding' semi-Pagans, who had been engaged in a protracted and violent struggle for ideological dominance and supreme political power.

This bitter conflict, and its resolution, have their own logic in broad socio-historical terms. That logic is again developed below in some detail, but one might just mention at this point the fact that while the French found it useful to exploit and even suscite factional rivalries, with a view to a cut-rate colonial conquest, they equally were concerned to contain factional antagonisms when imposing a cut-rate colonial administration. The French however were by no means in control of these social forces, however much they might seek to turn them to various uses. To understand these forces one returns to the crucial moment of colonial conquest – 1886 – and to the three principal characters whose careers ended (in one case) and effectively began (in the two others) in that year. Having introduced the principals, the presentation then reverts to a treatment of the socio-historical background, then again to the principals (each in turn), concluding with the denouement of 1886.

First of the principals to be introduced is the first to have met his death, the Warlord Lat Dior, leading representative of the semi-Pagan party in Wolof society. Lat Dior was above all a warrior chief and aristocrat whose power rested on the locally practised form of slavery, a predator on his non-Wolof neighbours but also (crucially) on his own people. He may be taken to incarnate the principle of armed force in assuring a ruler's authority, however much he found it tactically useful (on occasion) to seek legitimacy in a nominal commitment to Islam. He may also be regarded as the Wolof leader most implacably hostile to French imperialism, the most resolute in meeting force with force.

Second of the principals is the starkly contrasted figure of Amadu Bamba, the Saint, a truly charismatic Muslim hero. Amadu Bamba did have his connections with the warlord elite in general, and with Lat Dior in particular, but he specifically repudiated both their semi-Pagan beliefs and the violent methods by which they 'governed' their subjects. He was to have outstanding success as a Muslim missionary teacher and guide, a success owed in large part to the suppleness and realism with which he adapted his religious message to a theologically ignorant audience. He also, while again repudiating violence as a means of resistance to French intrusions, provided a basis for an unarmed and discreet resistance to French authority above all at an ideological level.

The third principal, the Knight, Shaikh Ibra Fall, is not only seen to have played the crucial part, but also that which was the least obviously predictable in terms of the social alignments of the time. Ibra Fall was regarded by many of his contemporaries as in some way 'mad', but his mental disequilibrium (if any really existed) was to be the basis of his own material success. It was also to play a large part in the growth and development of the religious movement which the Saint nominally led. Ibra Fall carried on the Warlord's tradition in practising and tolerating a very lax and heterodox form of Islam, and in using force to advance his aims. But he was also a most adaptable aristocrat, who recognised the need both to exclude the use of violence against the French and to accept Muslim (saintly) leadership as a desirable or even necessary concomitant of French peace.

The year 1886, in which the Warlord Lat Dior was killed in battle with a French column, and in which the Knight and later his retinue declared formal submission to the Saint, was the symbolic occasion of a social and cultural synthesis which proved explosive in its subsequent impact on Wolof society. The social synthesis of Muslim and semi-Pagan took place in a new Muslim brotherhood of a quite distinctive character. The success of this Mouride brotherhood is locally perceived today as a 'miracle', and by any secular standards it is indeed at least very remarkable.

A study of the three leading actors must not only treat their separate and contrasted historical roles, and the manner in which each came to represent a distinct leadership principle. It must also deal with the relations between them. Each at some point in his lifetime had important connections with the two others: the triangle is neatly drawn. These connections were furthermore popularly regarded as important, both during their lifetimes and since. The precise nature of the audience reaction has indeed gradually changed over time, in particular with the consolidation of Muslim leadership and a concomitant tendency to the 'purification' of what was originally a remarkably heterodox body of nominally Islamic belief. Today it has become generally distasteful to stress one's original connections with the pre-colonial Wolof chiefs, whose memory inspires little affection. Semi-pagan beliefs, even where they are still conspicuously present, are retained only with a growing defensiveness and even shame. These changes to some extent obscure the exact nature of popular sentiments, in particular where the role of two of the leading actors (Warlord and Knight) is concerned. But records kept by the colonial administration at the time of conquest, together with the various versions of these events in Wolof oral history, in the end provide a clear enough impression of the dramatic interaction between the principals and the chorus.[3] Vehement denials of the importance of the chiefly party or its leaders in these events are indeed, in their very vehemence, as useful an indication of popular feeling as the equally categorical assertions to the contrary. The apparently contradictory versions of the crisis are a logical part of its outcome. Warlord and Knight were indeed each crucially important, but in some circles it is no longer fashionable to say so.

CLASS, POWER AND BELIEF

Religion drew up the lines of battle in nineteenth-century Senegal, giving definition and purpose to the two rival groups engaged in the long, bitter struggle for power in Wolof society. In an important sense this was indeed a conflict of ruling ideologies, but equally there was a great deal more at stake than religious belief. Religion (belief and practice) was genuinely of primary importance to at least some of the actors, and to many others it served at least as a convenient badge to distinguish friend from foe. But the rival parties were also to be distinguished by divergent, and eventually incompatible, economic orientations. The

Muslim puritans grew in power with the development of a cash-crop (peanut) economy, while the semi-pagans relied on the previously-established sources of wealth – slave-trading, semi-nomadic pastoralism and (above all) the booty gathered in warfare. Factional struggle on a nominally religious basis acquired a further dimension insofar as it ultimately came to be a fight for the prize of political dominance. In this armed strife the contestants came increasingly to resemble one another as two predatory warbands. The struggle was not quite conclusively resolved before French conquest, but the French long before the final conquest had come to exert great influence on the course of events. Religion was not indeed particularly important to the French, whose local interests were those of businessmen rather than Christian crusaders: colonial policy was in any case dominated by the secular (*Laïc*) orientation of most senior officials. But the changing demands of trade, replacing a commerce in slaves with one in peanuts, made the fortune of the Muslim party (just as the Atlantic slave trade had originally made the fortune of the chiefly aristocracy). Pious Muslims might scorn the infidel 'Nazarene'; but they were also well attuned to the Nazarene's export policy.

The traditional slave-trading elite had originally been formed around the noble matrilineages of the Wolof states – Walo, Jolof, Baol, Saloum and (especially) Kayor. Kayor with its long coastline, and preferential access to the French trading posts, rapidly acquired a dominant position among these states: it was also to provide the scene for the dramatic crisis to be fully described below. The traditional nobility, and the chiefs who were 'chosen' from their ranks, enforced their authority (increasingly, with the development of the trans-Atlantic slave trade) through a warrior class of slave origins. The warrior slaves were originally selected for the reliability and deference which their lowly origins seemed to guarantee, but quite rapidly they effectively became a corps of Janissaries who themselves chose their own noble ruler and dictated his policy.[4] Power thus came to be based not on any 'traditional' legitimacy but on control of the means of coercion: warfare produced captives who were enslaved and sold to the Europeans, in return for horses (from the sixteenth century) and guns (from 1700). These improved means of coercion enabled the warbands to raid more effectively, and successful raids secured more horses and guns: a spiralling situation. The Atlantic export trade reached its height in the eighteenth century, but abolition of this market (in 1815) appears to have made the warbands even more predatory. Slave-trading continued with the Moors to the North of the Senegal river, but with a reduced profit margin demanding increased production. The rulers of the various states (Wolof and indeed non-Wolof) appear in general to have observed a form of gentleman's agreement: one did not sell one's own subjects, but one tolerated the occasional slave raids of neighbouring states in return for a reciprocal tolerance at another time. Kayor remained unusual, if not indeed unique in the area, insofar as its warrior aristocracy made a practice of capturing, enslaving and selling their own freeborn subjects.[5] Apart from slave-trading the Kayor aristocracy lived by what might best be called a protection racket, whereby the subjects paid 'taxes' for the service of not being enslaved, having their villages burned or their harvest taken. A principle of ruling authority was thus about as relevant to the ruler (Damel) of Kayor as to Al Capone in his heyday. The booty of war could be banked in the form of millet (the subsistence crop) and herds of cows which the aristocracy used to maintain themselves and their extensive clientele.

The semi-pagan warband, a group designated by the term *Tyeddo* which was variously applied to aristocrats in general or to 'pagans' in general, has been estimated at about one quarter of the total population – doubtless including the retinue with the aristocracy.[6] In the nineteenth century three quarters of their subjects were already Muslims. And whereas the aristocracy may have seen themselves as proud chevaliers (*Samba Linguer*), whose principal attributes were bravery and generosity, to their Muslim subjects they were simply drunken and impious extortionists. The Muslims did not indeed passively await their own enslavement, but soon found effective means of armed defence (and attack). Before dealing with this development in more detail, however, it may be necessary to further specify some of the cleavages of social class which divided the two factions – from each other, and also in each case internally.

Slavery was a long established institution in the Senegal area, dating back at least to the fifteenth century. The local term for slave (*Jam*) covers many distinct social conditions, but broadly (apart from the warrior *Tyeddo* who constitute a quite special case) the crucial distinction is that between the slaves of the aristocratic class (used for some menial tasks and always potentially for sale) and slaves of the Muslim farmers (providing labour for agricultural production). In either category they made up a very substantial proportion of the total Wolof population, somewhere between one and two thirds according to French estimates at the time of conquest. Where not put on the export market their local condition, while not that of the American plantation, was very far from idyllic. They were menials generally disregarded by their masters and liable to frequent physical punishment. On the other hand slaves always had the chance of upward mobility over generations, as is most dramatically illustrated by the case of the *Tyeddo*. But they did in general welcome French initiatives towards the abolition of local slavery, first in 1848 in the coastal 'colonies', then in 1905 throughout the Senegalese interior.[7] And whereas it may be generally true for West Africa that 'the emancipation of slaves by the colonial powers did not result in any kind of social upheaval',[8] this was not the case in Kayor where emancipation was one of the principal agents in the growth of the Mouride brotherhood. The slaves of Kayor were not happy men, but they knew when and how to seize a chance.

Occupationally specialised castes were dependent above all on the traditional courts, a retinue of artisans of various kinds as well as praise-singers. The generic local term for the castes (*Nyenyo*) still carries with it a strong sense of social disdain, and the principle of endogany (largely notional where other social classes were concerned) was in this instance rigidly enforced even within each distinct occupational category. The material condition of a casted person might often be better than that of many freemen (and was so especially in the case of the praise-singers) although he could not hope to escape his casted origins. The *Nyenyo* made up some one tenth of the total Wolof population, and together with the warriors and nobles they made up the backbone of the semi-pagan party: their livelihood depended on aristocratic affluence and patronage.

If the social composition of the semi-pagan party is in these terms broadly intelligible as one of aristocrats, clients and menials, that of the Muslim opposition again in general terms can be understood as the freeborn peasant farmers with the qualified support of their enslaved proletariat. These peasants formed their warbands under the leadership of militant Muslim reformers, with the avowed purpose of eliminating pagan survivals from local Islam. Particularly given their intransigent hostility to alcohol, this of course meant war with the *Tyeddo*. Holy war could also on occasion be directed against the French, but the latter's superior military power dictated a certain reticence here. In any case the first objective of Muslim puritans was to eliminate the local aristocracy, their matrilineally based form of social organisation, their devotional laxity and their oppression. Peanut revenue, from the mid nineteenth century onwards, enabled peasant producers to buy their own guns and fight the *Tyeddo* on equal terms. In some respects the Muslim party was socially revolutionary, especially given a notional claim to the equality of all Muslims at least before God. But the holy revolutionaries were not opposed to the institution of slavery as such, rather to the aristocrats' obnoxious practice of enslaving and selling them. Nor indeed, once effectively organised in warrior bands, were they averse to many of the despotic practices which originally they rejected. But to those whom they enslaved they also dictated a rigorous observance of all requirements of the faith, while organising these reformed slaves in small-scale units of agricultural production (ten to fifteen slaves per freeborn household). Given the technological limits in peanut production, and given the fact that the Muslim farmers did not (as did the *Tyeddo*) dissipate their profits in luxury spending (alcohol above all), this was probably as efficient a form of economic activity as the times and the available resources allowed.[9]

In the second half of the nineteenth century the armed attrition of rival parties in Wolof society went far enough to produce something like a Chinese warlord situation, an armed anarchy whose only law was that of the rapid rise and fall of particular leaders. In overall terms the Muslims undoubtedly gained, but still in the 1880s, Baol could be described as 'essentially a Fetishist state'.[10] And Baol, the eastern hinterland of Kayor, was to be the chosen area of colonisation of the Mouride brotherhood – built as it was on the debris of the semi-Pagan states.

France's concern with these dramatic (and for ordinary Wolof people often tragic) developments was of course very much more than that of the (interested) spectator. In earlier times (up to 1807) the French had been quite content to limit their interest to that of a trade with the established

Wolof courts, exchanging guns for slaves to the clear benefit of both trading partners. To protect their meagrely staffed coastal forts, they were also (despite occasional friction over precise terms) willing to pay an annual tribute (*Coutume*) to the Wolof rulers.[11] These established relations, viable if not cordial, were effectively destroyed by the final abolition of the trans-Atlantic slave trade (1815). The ruling courts had little enthusiasm for the substitute export commodity proposed by the French (peanuts), both because it enabled peasant subjects to escape their control and because the French eventually insisted on establishing an improved transport network which directly menaced the rulers' sovereignty. Muslims on the whole welcomed the new transport facilities in the interior ('the peanut railway'), but the peasants shared some of the courts' resentment where emancipation of slaves was concerned,[12] and also intermittently resisted French ambitions to impose colonial administration on the Wolof by armed force. Pre-conquest Wolof politics thus could remain a complex enough pattern of shifting alliances, as circumstances and individual ambitions dictated, between Muslim, semi-pagan and Nazarene. The French, fishing skilfully in these troubled waters, landed their catch with remarkably little exertion: Senegal became a colony at small financial cost to the French taxpayer and small human cost to the French military. The peasant farmers of the Muslim party could adjust to the new colonial situation, albeit with some sense of humiliation and with a degree of resentment at the modified conditions of indenture now required for the ex-slave labour force. The pagan party – aristocrats, clients and slaves – could not adjust without radical new initiatives in the whole pattern of their lives.

The Warlord

An excellent contemporary drawing of Lat Dior, now

preserved in Senegal's national archives, shows the physical profile of a brigand – almost to the point of caricature. Short in stature, substantial paunch enveloped in a wide cummerbund, a face more Arab than Negro in dominant features: long curved scimitar nose, wide curling lips, low receding brow and a baleful stare. The physical presence remains powerful, even sinister. Oral tradition, in any case still somewhat discordant where he and his like are concerned, gives little reliable information on his character – certainly there is no material for anything like a psychological interpretation. Descendants of his praise-singers emphasise his reputation for 'a great generosity', but 'generosity' was always incumbent on a man in his position. He was apparently sensitive to the taunts of his opponents about his physical size, once retorting that 'a man doesn't have to carry his kingdom around on his head'.[13] Such short stature, an attribute which of course in any case he shares with some other great military leaders, certainly did not inhibit impulses to physical aggression. And above all he was a man of pride, jealous of his own ruling position and of the independence of 'his' Kayor from any actual or potential threat. His obstinate intransigence in the circumstances of the times involved him in incessant armed struggle, and ultimately cost him both his ruling position and his life.

Lat Dior was born (c. 1842) into one of the seven noble matrileages of Kayor (the Guedji), eligible therefore to the position of Damel. He was first chosen as supreme ruler at the age of twenty, not indeed by the ostensibly traditional procedure of 'election' by his matrilineal peers but by the armed support of a faction of the warrior *Tyeddo*. And in this case the Cromwellian principle held good – 'the same arts that did gain a power must it maintain'. Non-stop warfare took up all Lat Dior's adult life, while recognised (effectively, by the French) as ruler of Kayor (1862–4, again 1871–82) and while excluded from power (1864–71,

1882–6). The enemy varied with circumstance, but the war remained equally bitter whether he be French, Muslim or a semi-pagan rival.

The military struggles which fill the whole period from 1862 to 1886, superficially contradictory in the sudden adoption of yesterday's opponent as today's ally (and vice versa) are quite consistent in character if one recalls the guiding principle of personal political power: and more than merely personal power, in so far as the stakes also involved the whole of Lat Dior's ambiguously subservient entourage. Against the French Lat Dior and his men developed tactics of attrition, so far as possible avoiding direct confrontation, which made the Wolof states the scene of a remarkably sophisticated and prolonged guerilla struggle – scorched-earth, tactical withdrawal imposing long and debilitating marches on the better-armed colonial troops and (when the time was ripe) ambush. With these tactics the Damel's troops scored two remarkable (if minor) victories against the French (in 1863 and 1865), though decisively beaten in two other encounters (in 1869 and 1886). Lat Dior's forces were also pitted against those of the Tukulor Muslim warrior Ahmadu Shaikhu of Podor, a holy war in which they were defeated in 1868, victorious in 1875. And on another occasion they were defeated by the pagan forces of the Serer state of Sine. Various ideologically divergent alliances were formed in these struggles: thus Lat Dior fought on one occasion together with the Muslim militants in holy war against the Pagans (1867), on another occasion together with the French against the Muslim militants (1875), and previously with the Muslims in holy war against the French. This whole chaotic pattern of changing alliances is only intelligible as one of expediency built around its single simple principle – me (and us) first.

Throughout his life the ruler, however proud of his

position and jealous of his independence, remained in fact dependent on the turbulent warband which had chosen him to rule and which then enforced his authority over the subjects while defending him from the various outside forces which threatened Kayor. There was however some tension between the warband, numbering some one thousand horsemen and three hundred foot-soldiers at the height of their power,[14] and their chosen ruler. The strain in this relationship can be dated from the moment (in 1864) when Lat Dior and his soldiers were compelled by circumstance to seek alliance with the powerful Muslim holy warlord Ma Ba. Ma Ba demanded of his new allies that they observe at least the external appearances of 'conversion' to Islam. Lat Dior was appointed principal military commander of the faithful but his followers suffered the symbolic humiliation of having their long tresses shaved. To be sure this was no more than a temporary humiliation. Ma Ba himself was soon killed in battle against the Pagans of Sine (1867), an encounter which his supreme commander discreetly left before its conclusion, and the armies of Kayor were then free to revert to the good old life of loot and booze. But the conversion, however formal and temporary, and however necessary to refugees from French expansion, continued to rankle. Some of the Damel's principal lieutenants never apparently forgave him for it, and were certainly to use their memory of the incident in justification of their desertion of the leader towards the end of his life. One of these lieutenants, Demba War Sall, was even to guide and accompany the French column which finally defeated and killed Lat Dior. Judas was suitably rewarded for his services: the French, while abolishing the office of Damel, then appointed Demba War as President of a new 'Confederation' of Kayor.

Lat Dior's struggle to preserve his power, while in various circumstances directed against many different local opponents, was always dominated by problems created directly or indirectly by French expansion. France was his principal and most dangerous enemy, and the Damel tenaciously opposed each new colonial encroachment on his power. As early as 1864 he refused to sanction a French project to establish a telegraph link across Kayor from Dakar to St Louis: this was the occasion of his first dismissal from office, enforced by a colonial military expedition. He tried to prevent his subjects from growing peanuts, firstly because the farmers used cash-crop revenue to buy guns with which they could effectively oppose him in the name of Islam, and secondly because France's interest in his lands was above all as a potentially productive agricultural zone. His diagnosis of the root of his problems was accurate enough – 'when there are no more peanuts the whites will go away and I will be complete master of the country'.[15] But the peanut was not so easily to be suppressed: local as well as external interests had their stake in its development. In 1877, when the French proposed to build a railway line along the route of the telegraph wire, Lat Dior again protested. His first reaction was one of simple derision – 'to send a steamship across dry land is as impossible as putting one bottle inside another'.[16] But when it became clear that the French really could accomplish this miracle, he and his warband attempted acts of sabotage along the tracks. This resistance, coupled with energetic protests – 'you are trying to cut my kingdom in two' – became increasingly desperate as its futility became more evident. The Damel's horse had a simple reaction on first seeing the railway line, appropriate for both horse and rider: it dropped dead. An armoured train dealt with saboteurs, forts protected those who came to sell their peanuts at the stations, the Damel himself was once more deposed and forced to flee from Kayor (1883).

Lat Dior went into exile in the hinterland with some four thousand followers, burning and looting as he went – above all, attacking the farmers and uprooting their peanut plants. His own circumstances rapidly grew desperate: first he 'lost' (in obscure circumstances) the vast herds of cows and sheep upon which his warband depended, then in their hunger the warriors suffered the supreme indignity: they were, as tradition records, 'forced to cultivate'. In these circumstances, and with prospects increasingly bleak, the less stubborn of his followers slipped away to make their own peace (or even alliance) with the French. Only three hundred remained to the last battle at Dekkile in 1886, when Lat Dior and seventy-five of his men were killed in an encounter with forty-five Spahis and two French officers. The colonial troops suffered no fatal casualties: for those contemplating armed opposition to the French, this was a final decisive demonstration of the full implications of the differential in military technology.

Today Lat Dior is remembered in some quarters as the hero of Senegal's early resistance to France. For his stand against the French he still inspires a certain pride among all Wolof, but oral tradition has not obliterated the memory of important contraditions in Wolof society at the time of conquest. The fact that crowds of enthusiastic farmers rallied to applaud the arrival of the first train at each new station along the railway line, the fact that colonial rule made possible a peaceful life for the first time in at least a generation, the fact that Islam was now to enjoy its full triumph, all these also are remembered. Lat Dior opposed the French among other things for their policy on slavery, and the archives have preserved his vehement letters of protest to St Louis on the emancipation of his refugee slaves in the coastal settlements: an interference with rights of property, or more simply, theft. However divided Wolof society had become, however, the collapse of the traditional state system in 1886 precipitated a further acute crisis even (and perhaps above all) for the victims of pre-colonial oppression. A whole political and military organisation died with the 'golden bullet' which allegedly killed Lat Dior. Aristocrats, clients, slaves, the semi-pagan party, were left deprived of their leader and their way of life. Pirates and victims alike needed a new leader who could show them a way out of the impasse.

The Saint

All the most salient features of Amadu Bamba's character present the most dramatic possible contrast to those of the semi-pagan Warlord. The Saint was a pious Muslim, peace-loving and ascetic, whose life was devoted to the improvement of his own religious knowledge and (at a much lower level) that of his followers. And he looked the saintly part: frail, thin, always clothed very simply in sandals, a long pure-white robe and white headdress which left only the eyes and nose uncovered.[17]

But if Amadu Bamba was an other-worldly saint, and the reputation has never been contested even by local opponents, his life was to be dominated by this-worldly events over which he had little or no control. Born in 1851, he grew up in the turbulent circumstances of pre-conquest warlordism. At the age of thirteen (in 1864) his family village was sacked and burned by soldiers of the Muslim warlord Ma Ba: his paternal grandfather (a Koranic teacher) was killed by the holy soldiers, while he and his father were deported to Ma Ba's capital at Nioro. In exile his father formed a close association with another unwilling guest, Lat Dior. Mamor Anta Selly quickly became the semi-pagan Warlord's principal 'Muslim adviser', and was to remain prominent in the Warlord's entourage after Ma Ba's death. He and his son returned in 1867 to the family village at Mbacké-Baol, where Lat Dior frequently made his camp: he married one of the Warlord's nieces. In 1871, when Lat Dior was allowed to return to Kayor, Amadu Bamba and his father went with him, and when the father died in 1880 the son remained in Kayor with a growing reputation for his scholarship and piety.

However contrasted the characters, there is thus a very significant if indirect connection between Saint and Warlord in their lives. Amadu Bamba did not follow his father's footsteps into the Warlord's entourage, he did not become an adviser, but he had been seen often enough with Lat Dior: this perceived connection was later to be a powerful factor in the growth of the Saint's following. Today the followers do not wish in general to emphasise any embarrassing debts to the semi-pagan past, and therefore repudiate anything their movement may have owed to Lat Dior. In so doing, they may sometimes exaggerate, but they are not merely adjusting yesterday's events to today's requirements. Amadu Bamba was repelled by the violence of his times, and he had as little affection for Lat Dior as for the holy warriors who had killed his grandfather: for him the rival warlords were quite simply 'men of murders and evil plots'. He is remembered as a champion of the poor and weak against their extortionate oppressors (certainly including Lat Dior) although he saw no solution in violent revolt.[18] His dislike for the semi-pagan ways of the old aristocracy was effective enough to provoke Lat Dior's son to pillage Mbacké-Baol once more in 1903, although more realistic and far-sighted aristocrats came to terms. The ruler of Baol in 1890, the ruler of Jolof in 1895, were to 'embrace Islam' and become his disciples – together with their retinues and many of their subjects. These 'conversions' were of no more than transient significance, as in each case they were quickly followed by the ruler's fall from office. It was another aristocrat, not a ruler, who was to make the decisive contribution to the Saint's troubled life.

By his own inclination, Amadu Bamba was above all a scholar, in the Sufi Muslim tradition, whose greatest desire was for the seclusion and tranquillity needed to read, to write, and to meditate. And despite the troubles of his life, he was certainly productive. Popular tradition credits him with having written no less than 'seven tons of books', weighty scholarship indeed, and in fact some forty-one (rather slim) volumes of his have been published. Thirty thousand lines of devotional poetry, four thousand of prose, all in an Arabic which although faulty is impressive enough for a man who taught himself virtually without assistance. The mere fact that a Wolof scholar could produce such quantities of verse in Arabic, without instruction or even much contact with those who spoke the language, is itself impressive. The work certainly cannot be admired for any independent quality: the Saint remains squarely in the Sufi tradition. F. Dumont in a recent extensive study of these writings finds 'nothing original' in all those thousands of lines[19] – on the contrary, a conscious avoidance of all originality, a rejection of the more extreme variants of Sufi mysticism, a traditionalist insistence on the transcendent Koran and *Sunna*. To the secular reader all this output may appear monotonous and derivative, repetitious and plain boring. But it should be remembered that to a man like Amadu Bamba 'originality' could be nothing else than a vice. His written work has a clear didactic purpose, it is to provide the basis for a campaign of mass education in Islam. The followers might not understand Arabic, though they could at least set the poems to music and 'sing' them at the top of their lungs, but there was an elite of Muslim scholars who could teach some basic religious principles using these texts.

The implementation of this missionary policy among illiterate semi-pagans amounted (as Dumont remarks) to not less than a cultural revolution.[20] Amadu Bamba took no active part in the work of proselytisation, but he endorsed the activists. The new disciples should submit themselves to 'the necessary guidance of a *Shaikh*', in the conventional Sufi Muslim phrase they should each be in his hands 'like a corpse in the hands of the washer of the dead'. The Saint sometimes helped to point his followers in the right direction in choosing a guide, but he could only warn them in rather elliptical terms that 'everything that seems round is not a cake, nor every light the moon'.[21] The disciples effectively chose their own 'necessary guides', who gave them a varying instruction in Islam but who in any case did promise salvation to the obedient. The Saint was realistic in recognising that the conversion of a great mass of semi-pagans could not be instantly effective in eradicating past belief and practise, but he was also realistic (as subsequent developments have shown) in believing that his writings could provide the basis for a steady drift in the direction of a purified Islam.

If the Saint's own missionary purpose was thus in large part realised, the more so since his own death (1927), it must be stressed that the disciples always saw their hero as very much more than a particularly well qualified Muslim teacher. And the qualities which they recognised in him were by no means necessarily even those of an exceptional Sufi saint (*Wali*). His initial charismatic revelation of 1891 is popularly held to have been a vision of 'the fish which holds up the world' – not an Islamic tradition.[22] Even the more cautious disciples still today maintain that their saint had 'a gift from God which you do not find in the Koran'. The less cautious ones quite simply addressed him as 'God' (*Allah*).[23] Such adoration, especially of course where it became an impious anthropolatry, seems to have spread despite Amadu Bamba himself and even against his stated wishes. For some disciples, he would be a God whether he liked it or not. The Saint continued to resent the turbulent crowds which sought him out, and both oral and written records bear witness to his frequent irritable outbursts to the besieging disciples. He was quite indifferent to the flow of pious offerings which he received – an other-worldly attitude not shared by the diligent relatives and assistants who appropriated his wealth. Amadu Bamba himself merely sought the seclusion necessary to his writing and meditation. He wanted to be left alone.

Apart from a genuine personal taste for solitude, the Saint had some good reasons to distrust the devotional fervour of his disciples. They brought him a lot of trouble, the vocal resentment of local chiefs whose authority was undermined, of fathers who lost a sturdy son to one of his pious settlements, of traders who saw their customers wasting good money on his holy offerings.[24] And above all the explosive growth of his following in the wake of the conquest cost him trouble with the French. Persecution at French hands without doubt was to contribute to the further growth of the Saint's following, but that might not have been anticipated and in any case could have given little comfort to the Saint in the time of his troubles. The French suspected a conspiracy to launch a new holy war, and to forestall this they forcibly dispersed the disciples in 1891, sent Amadu Bamba twice into exile, to Gabon (1895–1902) and to Mauritania (1903–7). French suspicions were certainly exaggerated where the Saint himself was concerned (and even the colonial authorities allowed a possibility of his innocence) but oral memory records that there were indeed disciples who also 'exaggerated' in urging the project of an anti-French *Jihad* on Amadu Bamba.[25] This project was most favoured by some leading members of the Wolof warbands, but the Saint remained vigorously opposed to any such use of force – distasteful, probably impious, and in any case doomed from the outset. He rebuked the pugnacious faithful in caustic language – the *Jihad* could only be justified for 'times which differed from yours, and whose men differed from yours'.[26] In the circumstances of the time, the faith could only expand peacefully – 'a holy war on souls'. But whatever the Saint's wishes, the semi-pagans found in his charismatic gift a consolation for the defeated Wolof nation. The dispersed warband found a new rallying point, so that the French apprehensively regarded the new disciples as 'a real army'.[27] The casted artisans came in the wake of their erstwhile patrons, and also, of course, came the slaves. Slaves of the pagan aristocracy probably were the preponderant element, at least in numerical terms. This was effectively guaranteed in the early years by the Saint's policy of accepting only those new recruits who declared themselves to be 'without relatives'.[28] Humane concern on the Saint's part was reinforced by fear of possible protests from the family.

There is no doubt that all this semi-pagan following alarmed the French, whose local agents persistently reported rumours of the purchase of weapons and plans for holy war. Fear of the Saint's 'dangerous' entourage prompted his double exile, but it was this persecution at French hands which established him securely as a true hero of Wolof nationalism. The talents of the entourage in the field of public relations found full expression in a gaudy (if derivative) mythology of the Saint's suffering: locked in a cell with a hungry (but of course miraculously pacified) lion, cast into a fiery furnace. All this and more he survived, and when he returned to Senegal it was held that only modesty prevented him from coming 'on wings'. Of the exile, Amadu Bamba's own writings record his principal complaint as his subjection to the unpleasant French custom of drinking coffee. But the public relations machine had its own momentum, and the mood of popular charismatic hysteria created a leader to its own specifications. If their hero had the miraculous power at any time to smite his tormentors, but chose in charity not to do so, this was thoroughly in accord with the popular feeling of the time.

French conquest was a humiliation (especially to the aristocracy) but it did also offer new possibilities (especially to the lower orders).

The Saint's own feelings where the French were concerned also had a genuine element of ambivalence. He certainly did not like them – 'O ye Jews and Nazarenes, die and do not hope for help tomorrow'[29] – but his dislike was less than hatred. Exile for him was less than torment, and there was certainly an element of sincerity in his proclamations of gratitude to God for providing him with peace and solitude. Although such statements were solicited by the colonial authorities, there was also truth in his pronouncement that 'by their government, the Prophet's religion has shone'.[30] French peace did indeed create the conditions for a further rapid diffusion of Islam, and of course for a spectacular growth of his own following. His own, reticent attitude is best symbolised in an encounter which he records with a French colonial officer. The administrator came and 'shouted' at him in a state of rage, while the Saint continued to recite prayers to himself: finally the Frenchman fell silent and 'his rage was calmed'. (It would be interesting to have the other source for that story.) Pride, reserve, obstinate withdrawal, all is there.

The Knight

Shaikh Ibra Fall, the powerful personality who provided a worldly solution to the predicament of the Saint's charismatic devotees, was above all things a man of ingenious versatility. His particular talent was to discover ways in which his own far-ranging material ambitions could be reconciled with the various (and changing) interests of his time. He could find something valuable to offer to virtually everybody – to the Saint, to the Warlord's following, and to the French – always, of course, at a price. In the interplay of our three leading roles, his is paradoxically enough the dominant part. It is also, as already remarked, the least readily predictable in terms of the prevailing ideologies and social forces of the time: Ibra Fall remains the joker in the pack. His characteristic versatility, and the ambiguity which surrounds his role, make him particularly difficult to label. In a previous essay he has been designated as 'the Squire'[31], with the intended connotation of some of the attributes of Squire Western – hard-drinking, hard-swearing, hard-riding. But such a label, however appropriate in these limited terms, does also jar in its suggestion of the relatively peaceful circumstances of post-feudal England. Ibra Fall lived in times when established social roles (of dominance or subjection) were quite suddenly and drastically called into question. A man of ambition in these circumstances did best by writing himself a new part. The label 'Knight' is preferred here for that part, for reasons which will emerge below, but it is recognised that no single label can be altogether appropriate to the rich diversity of the role.

Ibra Fall was born (*c.* 1858) into the warrior aristocracy of northern Kayor: reputedly he was a 'fairly close' (but imprecisely defined) descendant of an earlier Damel (Amadu Ngone Sobel). In appearance he was an archetypal representative of the *Tyeddo* warband: brightly coloured robe with a wide leather belt, hair worn in long tresses, great wooden club always to hand. A photograph survives showing a tall, powerfully built figure with a broad flat face: a photograph too poor in quality to show anything like a glint in the eye. The appearance is altogether impassive. A French administrator who interviewed him left with a rather different, disturbing memory of his 'twitches, his nervous giggles' and remarked on his convulsions with 'a sort of *delirium tremens*'.[32] (Shaikh Ibra by repute was greatly devoted to *eau-de-vie*.) The spectacle was apparently 'unattractive', and the administrator cautiously concluded that 'one would be tempted to take him for a simpleton'.

Many of Ibra Fall's Wolof contemporaries were more than just 'tempted', their first reaction on his arrival at the Saint's Muslim school in 1886 was to dismiss him as a 'madman'. Ibra Fall was certainly no ordinary disciple-pupil. On first seeing the Saint he dropped to his knees, removed all his clothes, and crawled naked to Amadu Bamba's feet: there he prostrated himself and declared his allegiance in words which have since become standard for a Mouride disciple – 'I submit to you in this world and the next. All that you order me I will do. Everything you forbid me I will abstain from doing.' This was the behaviour and mode of expression of a slave rather than a disciple, a semi-pagan rather than a Muslim idiom. The new follower went on to express his devotion to the Saint in a manner which effectively repudiated every requirement of Islam: he would not fast, he would not pray, but he did display an exuberant devotion in hard physical labour on the Saint's behalf. Tradition has it that Ibra Fall had already presented himself in a similar manner at the feet of several other notable holy men, only to discover that they were 'not the man he sought'.[33] Presumably the impious fellow had simply been sent on his way. Today the disciples maintain that Ibra Fall 'had known Amadu Bamba before they came into this world', and that Shaikh Ibra himself left these other holy men in disappointment. Amadu Bamba's decisive moment was first in hesitating to dismiss such an allegiance, then in deciding to accept on the new disciple's terms. Ibra Fall did indeed, like other *Tyeddo*, have a nominally Muslim background: his grandfather had apparently 'converted' to Islam, perhaps with the rest of the warband at the insistence of Ma Ba. But like other *Tyeddo*, he was faced in 1886 by the implications of defeat. He was however the first of the warband to see a way out.

Ibra Fall rapidly established a new pattern of behaviour

at the Saint's school, and his flamboyant subservience to the holy man did not inhibit his categorical rejection of the master's devotional practices. Prayer he scorned as a humiliation for a man of honour ('like begging'), the fast as an impediment to his daily labout ('too busy'), Muslim learning simply irrelevant ('not what I seek'). The Saint's first reaction to this scandalous attitude was simply to give the disciple a hoe and cutlass (the basic agricultural implements of the time), together with instructions in a single word – 'Go!' Whatever the Saint's intention, Ibra Fall did not take this for a dismissal. He grew millet for the disciples, cut wood and drew water, but he also remained in residence with the scholars whose material needs he served. At the same time he refused to tolerate anything less than abject subservience to the Saint, and frequently assaulted those scholars whom he regarded as having 'shown disrespect'. The scholars, understandably provoked, went to the Saint to demand that 'you get rid of your madman'. Amadu Bamba, presented with a simple choice ('him or us'), made a choice which still seems genuinely paradoxical in terms of his own pious background – however far-sighted it now appears in terms of a future diffusion of the faith. He chose the madman, with whom he left the school amid jeers from the pious scholars. This apparently inauspicious moment was effectively that of the foundation of the Saint's new Mouride brotherhood.

Saint and Knight, with only two other disciples, now established a new settlement in the wilderness of Baol, the future village of Darou Salam. Ibra Fall continued unrepentant to act the part of a pagan slave. Some informants today maintain that the Saint explicitly dispensed his new disciple from the normal requirements of the faith, and he certainly did so tacitly in effect. Ibra Fall quickly displayed his organisational and propagandistic talents at the new village, which became a centre for refugees from French authority: after a brief recruiting mission, the Knight returned with some seventy members of the Kayor warband. Here was a new form of Muslim movement, where the special talents of Saint and Knight proved quite complementary: as one Kayor disciple declared at the time, 'Amadu Bamba is the Greatest and Ibra Fall is his Prophet'.[34]

At Darou Salam the Knight came into his own, organising agricultural service for the warrior apprentices. Religion was of small significance to these recruits – as one informant declared impassively, 'if Shaikh Ibra was mad, then they all went mad like him'. Agricultural production, necessary to the survival of disarmed warriors, was organised by Ibra Fall in ostensibly pious production teams (the *Dara Muritu*). Here the warriors could be taught agricultural skills, rudimentary enough albeit, being organised in self-sufficient communities while allowing the Knight to appropriate part of the produce. In these circumstances of heroic and pioneering isolation, agriculture could be made almost a substitute for military service. The warband could thus save face while also making a (meagre) livelihood: and the work was the more acceptable as a service to a saintly hero which would be rewarded in the afterlife. As Shaikh Ibra categorically assured the new disciples, 'each will go to paradise according to his work'. The Saint himself, having opted for his 'mad' Knight, took no further direct part in these proceedings, although doubtless he could regard it all as a further victory for the faith.

Agricultural labour was necessary first to the warband simply as a matter of survival (even Lat Dior had previously been 'forced to cultivate'). And the same dire exigencies of course also applied to the aristocrats' retinue, the slaves and artisans who flocked in the wake of their erstwhile masters to the new sacred farms. But the French had opened up new material opportunities through their encouragement of cash-crop agriculture (peanuts) in place of a subsistence economy (millet). There were financial possibilities in the new settlements, money of course in the first place for the organisers. The Saint might proclaim his quite sincere disinterest in 'the things of this world'. The Knight, especially after his formal liberation from the Saint's service (*c.* 1891) made no such claim on his own account. The French administrator who interviewed him at the town of Thiès found that he had 'been attracted, so he said, by the agricultural value of the land around'. By that time (*c.* 1912) he had about one thousand farming disciples of his own, and an annual income estimated at fifty thousand francs.[35] His numerous wives and chosen followers had been put in charge of trading posts along the railway line, buying peanuts and selling a range of imported goods (cloth, tea, etc.). He attracted attention for his 'keen business sense and opportunism', which among other things involved him in 'much commercial litigation'.[36] In the way of business he learned to make good use of the railway which Lat Dior had fought so bitterly, and in 1929–30 his followers even built their own railway, a thirty mile branch line to the saintly capital at Touba. Above all things he appreciated the new value which improved transport could confer on previously remote and isolated areas, and in 1918 he secured rights from the colonial government over an area of more than twenty square miles close to Touba. He had 'delivered' one hundred and fifty disciples as volunteers for the French army. When the first world war was over the French commandant summoned Shaikh Ibra to offer him the formal gratitude of the authorities: the Knight's plain-speaking reply is remembered by his sons – 'thanks, that's all very well, but I want land'.

Land to the Knight meant money, and his quick perception was to realise that under colonial rule money would replace violence as the decisive instrument of aristocratic ambition. Cash could of course maintain a suitably extensive clientele, but it had many other uses. It could serve to buy valuable political protection. First, from the chiefs who acted as the subordinate local intermediaries of colonial authority (and Ibra Fall, married to two of Lat Dior's daughters, enjoyed 'very close relations with the principal chiefs').[37] Second, from the elected Deputy of Senegal's communes: Ibra Fall helped to finance the electoral campaigns of François Carpot, who held Senegal's seat in the French National Assembly from 1902 to 1914. Carpot returned the favour by twice successfully interceding to secure the Saint's return from exile (at a fee of ten thousand francs on one occasion, according to French police sources).[38] Third, according to oral sources if not police files, protection or at least sympathetic understanding from the French themselves: the relevant police file notes Ibra Fall as 'very intelligent' and 'deferential to authority' (this latter the highest reference of all under colonial rule). The French might consider Ibra Fall 'morally worthless', but they did add the perhaps complementary judgment that he was 'a subtle diplomat'.[39] In 1906, while addressing a moving plea to the Governor General for the Saint's return from exile, he did not fail to add his own characteristic touch, a note requesting a French decoration for himself.[40]

Shaikh Ibra Fall knew all the things that money could buy (women, good liquor, politicians) but he had none of the true capitalist's interest in money for itself. His genius was in a combination of talents – for work (with which he was in his early days 'obsessed' according to one of his sons), for political and commercial intrigue, and perhaps especially for organisation. The Saint's following, recruited initially from the wreckage of the state of Kayor, had many of the chaotic features of the true charismatic community. But Ibra Fall ensured that the disorganised were taken in hand, that they were soon settled in farming communities throughout the wilderness of Baol. A discreet but possibly decisive element of violence was required here, to guarantee security of tenure to the settlers. Here Ibra Fall came into his own as the Teutonic *Knecht* of what was to be quite literally the *Drang nach Osten* of the pagan party of Kayor. Conditions of indenture were indeed severe for those who struggled eastwards under the guidance and protection of Knights such as Ibra Fall, but they did need leadership to succeed in displacing the local Fulani pastoralists (Slavs to the Wolof Teutons).

A single example, unusual only in that it was the occasion of a French official investigation, may serve to illustrate the conditions of this Wolof colonisation. This encounter took place at the Fulani camp of Ngonga, a pastoral centre on the fringe of the area allocated to Ibra Fall by the French authorities. One morning in 1936, at the onset of the sowing season, over one hundred young male disciples invaded the camp (of a few families, some thirty persons in all). In the ensuing struggle fifteen Fulani were injured, nine seriously enough to be hospitalised. The Wolof disciples (of whom only one was hurt) then cut the throats of the cows and beat up the pregnant wife of the Fulani chief, who aborted. The Fulani lodged an official protest at the loss of their livestock and traditional grazing lands, and a local court served arrest warrants for nine of the Wolof (not apparently those who were in fact guilty, but those whom Ibra Fall's son judged 'dispensable'). Mamadu Mustapha Fall, who had ordered the invasion, reassured his disciples – 'we are in white man's country and I can always save you because I have money'. And he kept his word. The Governor of Senegal overruled the local verdict and declared the Fulani categorically in the wrong. The Falls well know the value of good friends in high places.[41]

The Knight's career may be entirely logical in terms of his own material ambitions: he died wealthy, master of thousands of acres and at least as many disciples, his many wives including the cream of Wolof nobility, effectively almost a Damel in his own right. An important puzzle however remains, in the relation between such a man of resolute, unflinching impiety and the men of Muslim scholarship who allowed such an associate freedom of action on his behalf. Ibra Fall of course initially presented himself as the Saint's 'slave', but he soon made it clear that his notion of such a relationship was the ambiguous subjection of a *Tyeddo* warband leader to his chief – and that allowed plenty of scope for private initiative. The Saint could accept such an allegiance no doubt in part because the Knight was a gifted propagandist, the Saint Paul who spread his master's word among the semi-pagans. One French authority on Amadu Bamba has diffidently concluded that the Saint himself had but a small part in the foundation of his own new brotherhood: 'one might almost say that the "brotherhood" of Mourides created itself'. True up to a point, given the social crisis of the time, but less true than a similarly diffident Mouride verdict: 'you might say that Shaikh Ibra Fall had the revelation of a separate Mouride way before Amadu Bamba himself'.[42] The Knight ensured that the Saint's miracles would not pass unnoticed, and for services of this kind he is today remembered by the nickname 'Lamp' (through whose radiance, as is said, the Saint became known).

Public notoriety, even as a Muslim hero, was nonetheless in itself rather less than a welcome gift to Amadu Bamba. The Saint was only too well aware of the problems attendant on his fame – trouble with the French, trouble with an avaricious entourage, trouble with the material demands of the disciples themselves. And it was amid all this less than holy disturbance that Ibra Fall made himself invaluable to his master. He could organise farming communities for the new semi-pagan disciples to whom the Saint would only address a single dismissive phrase – 'Go and work!' He could cater for the material needs of the Saint's demanding relatives, allocating money and labour service where required. By taking charge of the material world, he gave the Saint the peace and solitude he required to write his voluminous devotional works. The relation of Knight to Saint was thus that of a grey eminence dominating the material world to which the man of religion ostentatiously turned his back.

Ibra Fall did of course also give service to the Saint in acting as intermediary with the French, although his role in this connection may be more questionable. His intercessions (letters, pleas, and bribes) with administrators and politicians appear to have helped to bring about the Saint's return from both his exiles (1902, 1907). But it does also appear to be the case that the Knight's conduct helped in each case to get the Saint sent into exile in the first place. French fears of a possible holy war were founded above all on the observed behaviour of Ibra Fall's *Tyeddo* associates, many of whom sought to keep their weapons as well as their belligerent attitudes. The Saint publicly warned the Knight on one occasion (1903) 'to expel your bad disciples and keep only those who bring no trouble', and much later (1911) it was again reported that due to the unruly behaviour of certain disciples 'Ibra Fall is on bad terms with his master'.[43] But the Knight was never formally disavowed, and the Saint seems overall to have accepted his troubles as the price of taking over the (perhaps nominal) leadership and (in the long run) spiritual guidance of his originally semi-pagan flock. So one returns to the theme already discussed, that of the conditions of mass conversion to Islam. Amadu Bamba could legitimately view his tribulations as a (perhaps necessary) part of a triumph of the faith, the semi-pagans now placed under the guidance of spiritual superiors who could instruct them in the requirements of religion. The Knight may have won his own material reward for collaboration in this process, and may also effectively have shaped the material organisation of the faithful, but on balance his services to the Saint were worth the price.

1886: Decisive encounters

The threads of this story, and the roles of the three principals, are drawn together in the encounters which took place in the state of Kayor in 1886. Lat Dior, on the morning of his last battle at Dekkile, sought out Amadu Bamba to get his blessing[44] – 'I want to have done with the white men at all costs today.' The Saint, doubtless well aware of the probable outcome of battle with the French, and in any case unenthusiastic for such warlike endeavours, would merely consent to pray for Lat Dior 'so that peace may return'. Only his death could allow Lat Dior 'to have done with the white men', and the Saint at least gave him a suitably inscribed robe to be killed in – a one-way ticket to paradise. With the battle fought and predictably lost, it was Ibra Fall's turn to seek out the Saint: traditional accounts are reticent as to the Knight's presence at Dekkile, but if he were there he would certainly have left early.

The Knight's submission to the Saint has since acquired a great symbolic significance, as the submission of the dead Warlord's semi-pagan following to new and more rigorously Muslim leadership. The Knight's versatile talents also however made the significance of the occasion rather more than 'symbolic' – more than a representation of the submission of one social group (and ruling ideology) to another. Here, effectively was an instant routinisation of saintly charisma, an immediate adjustment of devotional hysteria to material survival and success. The functions of charismatic hero and worldly organiser were thus in this case to be separated and discharged by two different (but in terms of their attributes, complementary) persons. Such a separation seems a recurrent feature of new and revolutionary religious movements (Christ and Saint Paul, obviously, also for example the 'prophet' and the 'organiser' in the various Melanesian 'Cargo Cults' studied by Peter Worsley).[45] The pattern although frequently repeated is not of course universal: the two characteristic roles have also in other instances been combined in a single person (Muhammad). In the case of this study the complementary features of the alliance of Saint and Knight provided a very attractive solution (both ideological and organisational) to the leaderless Wolof semi-pagans. And the Warlord's death, which left the semi-pagans without their leader, was the appropriate dramatic moment for such a new synthesis. One of the principals had to leave the stage before the two others could play out their full parts. The golden bullet which despatched Lat Dior at Dekkile, in announcing the end of warlords and warlordism, also introduced a new social drama in the Mouride brotherhood.

NOTES

1 K. Marx, 'The Eighteenth Brumaire of Louis Bonaparte'. The sentence in full of course reads as follows. 'Men make their own history, but they do not make it just as they please, they do not make it in circumstances chosen by themselves, but under circumstances directly encountered, given, and transmitted from the past.' In Marx and Engels, *Selected Works*, London: Lawrence and Wishart, 1962, Vol. I, p. 247.

2 P. Marty, *Les Mourides d'Amadou Bamba*, Paris: Leroux, 1913, p. 120.

3 The colonial documentation used here is collected in the *Archives Nationales, Section Outre-Mer*, Paris (A.N.S.O.M.) and in the *Archives de la République du Sénégal*, Dakar (A.R.S.D.). Oral history from interviews conducted in Senegal, 1966–7.

4 On the rise of the *tyeddo*, see V. Monteil, *Esquisses Sénégalaises*, Dakar: Institut Fondamental d'Afrique Noire (I.F.A.N.), 1966, especially the essay on Lat Dior; also M. Klein, *Islam and Imperialism in Senegal. Sine-Saloum 1847–1914*, Edinburgh: Edinburgh University Press, 1968.

5 The principal source here is the invaluable report of the French traveller Mollien, a careful and perceptive observer who travelled through Kayor and the surrounding region after an epic escape from the famous shipwreck of the *Méduse*. G. T. Mollien, *L'Afrique Occidentale en 1818*, Paris: Calmann-Lévy, 1967 (first published in 1820), pp. 39, 48, 51, 75, 103. A very useful comparative review of slavery and trade in various West African societies is provided by C. Meillassoux in the excellent introduction to his edited volume, *The Development of Indigenous Trade and Markets in West Africa*, London: Oxford University Press, 1971.

6 M. Klein, 'Revolution and Social Change in Nineteenth Century Senegambia', Toronto (n.d.), p. 7 (typescript).

7 On the implementation of anti-slavery legislation, see M. Guèye, 'L'Affaire Chautemps (Avril 1904) et la suppression de l'esclavage de case au Sénégal', in *Bulletin de l'I.F.A.N.* Vol. XXVII, Série B, Nos. 3–4, 1965.

8 Meillassoux, p. 65.

9 M. Klein, 'Slavery, the Slave Trade, and Legitimate Commerce in Late Nineteenth Century Africa', in *Etudes d'Histoire Africaine*, Vol. II, 1971, p. 24, and Meillassoux, p. 66.

10 A. Le Chatelier, *L'Islam dans L'Afrique Occidentale*, Paris: Steinheil, 1899, p. 263. This work, apparently written in 1888, is a very useful report on a journey through northern Senegal at that time.

11 The best source on eighteenth-century trade is A. Delcourt, *La France et les Etablissements Français au Sénégal (1713–1764)*, Dakar: I.F.A.N., 1952. This trade of course did involve commodities other than just guns and slaves (Gum Arabic exports, alcohol imports, etc.).

12 Capt. Brosselard, *Rapport sur la Situation de la Vallée du Sénégal en 1886*, Lille: Danel, 1888, pp. 28–9.

13 On Lat Dior, see V. Monteil, *Esquisses Sénégalaises . . . op. cit.;* also G. Ganier, 'Lat Dyor et le Chemin de Fer de l'Arachide', *Bulletin de l'I.F.A.N.* Vol. XXVII, 1965; and the published translation of a notable praise-singer's account, A.M. 'Samb', *Cadior Demb*, Dakar: Imprimerie Diop, 1964. Samb's version of the Warlord's career leaves a rather different and more favourable impression than the accounts given by any of my Wolof informants.

14 Ganier, p. 231.

15 Monteil, p. 95.

16 *Ibid.* p. 99.

17 For a French administrator's contemporary account of the character of the Saint and his religious following, see P. Marty, *Les Mourides . . .;* for a study of the Saint's writings, F. Dumont, 'Essai sur la Pensée Religieuse d'Amadou Bamba', *Thèse de Doctorat*, Université de Dakar, 1968; also D. Cruise O'Brien, *The Mourides of Senegal*, Oxford: Clarendon Press, 1971, esp. pp. 37–57.

18 One interviewee, Mouhamadou Diakhaté of Touba, stressed the Saint's sense of distance from the leaders of the time very simply; 'he was the first Muslim leader not to carry a gun, only his pen'.

19 F. Dumont, 'Essai sur la Pensée Religieuse d'Amadou Bamba . . .', p. 565. Dumont's study, which most unfortunately remains unpublished, not only includes the first extensive translations of the Saint's poetry but also

consistently relates these writings to the various Sufi sources and to other comparable material.

20 Dumont, p. 567. Dumont identifies the Saint's writing overall as no more than 'a work of popularisation' (p. 566).

21 *Ibid.* p. 364.

22 P. Des Isles, 'Contribution à l'Etude du Mouridisme', St Louis (Senegal): 1948 (unpublished).

23 The 'cautious' version is from an interview with Ainu Sèye (Touba). The less cautious from French sources: although no disciple today calls the Saint a God, it is remembered that some disciples once did (Interview, Sérigne Mbacké Nioro, Missirah).

24 Letters of complaint (from chiefs, relatives, traders) are preserved in *Dossier Amadou Bamba* (D.A.B.), A.R.S.D.

25 The Saint's possible innocence of intent to mount a holy war is mentioned in *Rapport Merlin*, 29 Aug. 1895, A.N.S.O.M., Sénégal, IV, 127. French suspicions of the entourage in this connection were confirmed by a number of interviewees at Touba in 1966–7.

26 *Fatwa* of 1910, in D.A.B., A.R.S.D.

27 *Rapport Leclerc*, 15 Aug. 1895, A.N.S.O.M., Sénégal, IV, 127.

28 The Saint's refusal to accept those 'with relatives' was stated in interview by Ainu Sèye: it has taken me some time to appreciate the implications of this policy.

29 *Fatwa* of 1912, in D.A.B., A.R.S.D.

30 Ode to Governor-General William Ponty, 1913, in A.N.S.O.M., Afrique Occidentale Française, XVIII, 8.

31 D. Cruise O'Brien 'The Saint and the Squire', in C. Allen and W. Johnson (eds.), *African Perspectives,* Cambridge: Cambridge University Press, 1970.

32 Marty, p. 28. French sources provide some useful material on Ibra Fall, but the account here is based above all on interviews. Moussa Sall, as the 'official historian' of the Fall family, gave a particularly full account, supplemented notably by Baay Diao, Aliyu Fall, Sérigne Mbacké Nioro and Moussa Sarr. But every Mouride, disciple or saint, has his own view to give on Shaikh Ibra Fall.

33 Amadu Bamba's 'first disciple' Adama Guèye, by repute both illiterate and particularly 'stupid', brought Ibra Fall to the Saint after 'many great *marabouts*' had been found wanting.

34 Marty, p. 44.

35 Marty, p. 28. Figures from *Fiche de Renseignements, Ibra Fall*, n.d., in A.R.S.D. 13G 68. This '*Fiche*', one of many kept by the colonial administration on Muslim notables, includes much useful material doubtless provided by anonymous police informers.

36 Marty, pp. 28–9.

37 *Fiche de Renseignements, Ibra Fall* . . . Ibra Fall had a great many wives and concubines (he drew little distinction between 'married' and 'unmarried'), and even the 'wives' numbered far in excess of the four permitted in Islam.

38 Unsigned note, 19 Nov. 1912, in D.A.B., A.R.S.D.

39 *Fiche de Renseignements.*

40 Shaikh Ibra Fall to Governor General, 29 Nov. 1906, in D.A.B., A.R.S.D.

41 French documentation on the Ngonga incident in A.R.S.D., 13G 43. Ibra Fall himself, who died in 1930, was not of course involved in this particular skirmish, but the local Fulani remember similar invasions in Ibra Fall's lifetime. The Ngonga incident is true to the Knight's tradition, and is chosen from other similar incidents in view of the particularly copious documentation which it provoked.
42 F. Dumont, p. 125, and Sérigne Mbacké Nioro (interview).
43 Governor-General of French West Africa to Minister of Colonies, *Rapport 1911* (7 Sept. 191, , in A.N.S.O.M., Sénégal, I, 97 quat.) The Saint's open letter of 1903 in D.A.B., A.R.S.D.
44 A detailed and altogether believable account of this meeting is given in A.M. 'Samb', *Cadior Demb*, Dakar: Imprimerie Diop, 1964, p. 54.
45 P. Worsley, *The Trumpet Shall Sound,* London: Paladin Edition, 1970, pp. 327–8 (first published 1957).

2

LAND, CASH AND CHARISMA

LAND, CASH AND CHARISMA

An economic sociology of the Mouride brotherhood

INTRODUCTION: A MYTH OF EXPLOITATATION

The saints of the Mouride brotherhood (the spiritual heirs to Amadu Bamba and his associates) have consistently been portrayed by outside observers as a holy aristocracy enjoying great material privileges through the economic exploitation of some half a million poor peasant disciples. The disciple is promised his reward in the next world, and paradise is purchased from the saint by work in his service and by more or less regular cash instalments. The saintly vehicle of salvation sits back and enjoys the profits. The brotherhood as a whole, with its elaborate hierarchy of saintly authority, then becomes in caricature no more than an unusually successful variant of a familiar type of sacred confidence trick.

This is caricature, certainly, but one which remains quite plausible to the secular mind. The more successful saints do display their wealth with ostentation. The Citroën, Mercedes-Benz, Chevrolet, are commonplace enough sights in and around the brotherhood's capital at Touba. The saintly houses, at which these limousines are parked, are large and sumptuous by local rural standards – though generally inferior to the residences even of middle-level civil servants in Dakar. Fine clothes, expensive French perfumes, a retinue of servants, young and beautiful concubines, complete the picture of a luxury which is striking enough when set against the poverty of a local peasant family with its average annual income (per head) of some twenty pounds. The gigantic mosque of Touba, which cost at least a million pounds to build, is an appropriate symbol of this apparent exploitation.

Such conspicuous wealth among the saints is the more remarkable when one recalls that it is ultimately based on the disciples' devotion to the cultivation of peanuts, a crop seldom associated with any notable economic success. Saintly revenue comes from a few large estates cultivated on a full-time basis by an elite of unremunerated followers, from a large number of fields cultivated part-time by villagers, from gifts and tribute based for the most part on peanut revenue, and only in small proportion from urban commercial speculation. There can be no doubt that the Mouride saints have succeeded in doing surprising things with peanuts.

There is, equally clearly, much superficial justification for the analysis and interpretation of the Mouride brotherhood as a system of socio-economic exploitation. Such a view has been dominant in a voluminous literature on the subject since the pioneering study of Paul Marty in 1913, notably in the various administrative studies and reports which rely on Marty's research (with or without acknowledgment).[1] In its most extreme form, as expressed for example in the 1952 report of Roland Portères, the brotherhood is seen simply as a resurrection of the traditional Wolof institution of slavery.[2] An alternative, which remains popular in the rhetoric of some Senegalese politicians and which has been adopted in a recent study by Lucy Behrman, is to regard the saints as 'feudal lords'.[3] The consensus in any case, in those studies which are directly concerned with Mouride economics, is that this is exploitation. Those authors who recognise a positive service provided by the saints see this above all in religious terms – Muslim teaching, the assurance of paradise.[4] None of the many studies on the subject, it seems to me, have properly understood (or in some cases even recognised) the positive *material* services which the saints have provided for their disciples. Yet the remarkable success of the brotherhood as a mass movement (some 700,000 brothers in 1973) and the material success of the saints, cannot be adequately explained without such an understanding.

The prevalent view of the brotherhood, at least in its dominant emphasis, now seems to me to be quite simply wrong. Misinterpretation springs in part from a vulgar Marxism as expressed in the writings of colonial administrators or post-colonial 'developmentalists'. It must be acknowledged that my own understanding of Mouride economics was initially influenced by views of this kind, especially at the time of my fieldwork (1966–7), but my understanding has since been altered for a number of reasons.[5] Firstly, new research (in the form of a series of monographic studies on Mouride villages) has provided a wealth of statistical information on land and labour in the Mouride zone. (The results do confirm the broad conclusions which I had earlier reached on a more impressionistic basis, but statistics are an improvement on informed guesses[6].) Secondly, it has taken time for me to understand fully the relation between aspects of my own research which were to some extent 'compartmentalised' into separate chapters for presentation in book form:[7] such relations were indeed mentioned throughout the text where relevant, but not drawn together in a comprehensive analytical statement at any one point. Thirdly, it has also taken time for me to grasp the full implications of certain inconsistencies between the statements of Mouride informants and their observed actions. The second and third considerations, in particular, for some time obscured my understanding of the relation between religious loyalty and the pattern of land settlement over the past half century. And it is this relation which I now see as crucial.

Misunderstanding of the brotherhood, the apparently plausible conclusion that the saints have mercilessly exploited the credulity of their peasant disciples, seems paradoxically to derive in part from the disciples' own description of their situation. The loyal *talibé* characteristically declares that he works for his saintly superior, and gives his religious offerings, solely in the expectation of an other-wordly reward – 'for paradise alone'. He asks and expects nothing here below. He also declares his readiness to obey the saint in any instruction which the latter may give. Secular observers, and indeed non-Mourides in general, have taken such declarations as a positive affirmation by the victims of their own exploitation and subjection. This seems the obvious secular translation of the disciples' view, but it leads to an erroneous conclusion for one simple but superficially bizarre reason. The disciple, in affirming his exploitation and subjection, is distorting the reality of his social and economic situation. In his own devotional language, he is in fact boasting. (I should acknowledge here a debt to my interpreter Thierno Sow, a somewhat sceptical Mouride, who remarked after leaving a disciple who had just given a detailed and moving account of his life service to his saint – 'he's only boasting'.)[8]

Boasting in varying degrees, certainly, but always boasting nonetheless. And it is logical enough that the disciple should wish to do so, in terms of the doctrine which the saint proclaims and which the loyal disciple must at least appear to accept. The declaration of allegiance, which is made by all disciples, is an engagement of total obedience to the saint 'in this world and the next'. Obedience in this world implies various forms of tribute, in labour, in kind, and in cash. This tribute in turn is ideologically justified by the disciples' access to the saint's charismatic powers of redemption (*baraka*), and by that alone. But Mouride ideology, however logically coherent on its own terms, in fact serves to conceal or disguise important aspects of the real relation between the saint and his disciple.[9] The latter is in the first place often by no means as unconditionally loyal and obedient as he maintains: there is a real reservation beneath the ostentatious subjection, as any detailed examination of his actions will reveal.[10] In the second place, and more importantly for the argument here, there is an expectation of material as well as spiritual reciprocity. The material success of the saints is only fully intelligible in terms of their success in providing material services to the disciples. These services have been political as well as economic, under the colonial and post-colonial state, but the argument of this essay will effectively be restricted to economic considerations (Mouride politics being separately treated below, particularly as a part of the analysis in 'Clans, clienteles, and communities').

The key to an understanding of the economic successes of the brotherhood as a whole, and of the saints in particular, lies in the organisation which the saints have provided for a mass movement of agrarian settlement. The Mourides, over the past half century or more, have established farming communities throughout a vast zone (thousands of square miles) of hitherto uncultivated land around the fringe of Senegal's central desert (the Ferlo). This massive agrarian colonisation has involved an evolution of social and economic organisation, from the original pioneer settlements to the constitution of village communities. The economic life of the brotherhood must therefore be understood as a historical process, which is analysed here in terms of two basic type situations – that of the holy pioneer and that of the peasant villager – with a note on a third and increasingly significant type, that of the urban migrant.

Each of these 'type-situations', as will be shown, does involve a degree of economic exploitation (or unequal exchange) in secular terms, but the process as a whole should be seen quite differently. The Mouride brotherhood has historically been a vehicle of economic emancipation, and of a relative social advancement, for recruits drawn in large proportions from the most disadvantaged sectors of pre-colonial Wolof society (slaves in particular, also the despised artisanal castes). Under the umbrella of French colonial rule, and under saintly leadership, these lower orders of the Wolof hierarchy achieved something like a covert social revolution. As with other revolutions, there were also victims, in this case the pastoral Fulani who lived along the desert fringe. The organisation which assured the economic emancipation of some secured it at the expense of the means of livelihood of others.

SACRED PIONEERS

The great wave of Mouride agrarian settlement (as we have seen) was originally set in motion by the conditions of social and economic crisis occasioned by the imposition of French colonial rule in the Wolof zone. The pre-colonial Wolof system, devoted to slave-trading and to pastoral herding often on a very large scale, had relied on a mass of unfree labourers generally designated as slaves (*jam*). And these slaves were, of course, liberated by colonial rule, a liberation applied with increasing effect by the end of the nineteenth century. Freedom from their masters did not however provide increased economic security, often indeed the contrary. The specialised occupational castes or *nyenyo* (blacksmiths, carpenters, etc.) also suffered not only from the competition of French manufacturers but also from colonial sanctions against their aristocratic patrons. Slaves and castes shared a common predicament in the marginality or non-existence of their rights to land in the traditional zones of Wolof agricultural settlement.

Land in these areas was already overcrowded by the late

nineteenth century, especially so in the region of Kayor. Improved medical services under French rule appear to have been partly responsible for a demographic explosion which in turn tended to result in overcultivation and then in exhaustion of the soil. Land hunger was a natural result of this process, and it was to be expected that the principal victims should turn their attention to the hitherto uncultivated 'new lands' of the Ferlo fringe – the hinterland of Kayor. The urgency of the search for new land was compounded by the imposition of a head tax which could only be paid with the cash proceeds of peanut farming. It also seems that the remote and inaccessible lands of the Ferlo fringe had a special appeal to those who sought to escape the vigorous French military recruitment drives, or indeed to escape payment of the head tax.

The colonial government, despite such efforts to evade its authority, was on the whole disposed to encourage settlers in their pioneering endeavours. Mouride settlers in particular soon acquired a reputation (later, a notoriety) for an almost obsessive devotion to the cultivation of peanuts. And the peanut, as the French had recognised by the mid nineteenth century, was the crop which alone could make the colony of Senegal a paying proposition. France provided a communications infrastructure throughout northern Senegal for the transport and marketing of the peanut crop. Railway lines in particular served to open up new lands in the hinterland regions of Baol, Jolof and Saloum.[11] Mouride pioneers in these regions were then able to build dust tracks across the savannah to link their settlements with the nearest rail station. The colonial government gave every assistance to the settlers, who seemed unequivocally progressive in converting a hitherto pastoral (and non-remunerative) zone into one devoted to cash-crop farming. Huge land grants were accorded to the Mouride saints, and the tiresome complaints of the previous inhabitants (the cow Fulani) either ignored or summarily dismissed by the French administrative authorities. Later (after 1945) the pioneering process was further assisted by a programme for tarred roads through the new lands, and by the provision of a series of bore-holes in the same drought-prone zone. Cash-crop production in all these circumstances became *possible* in the new lands, but one should not overlook the extent to which it also became positively *desirable* to grow peanuts. New articles of consumption became habitual, luxuries became necessities, and the good life (tea, sugar, cigarettes, etc.) was something that only peanuts could buy.

The motive for agrarian colonisation was strong, especially so among the lower Wolof classes. The opportunity to settle new lands had been created by the French administration. But these lands still remained an arid wilderness, difficult of access, with a dangerous non-human fauna (lions, notably) and a still more dangerous presence in the nomadic pastoral Fulani. Those who wished to seize the opportunity, in these circumstances, needed to be organised and to be fairly numerous: an isolated pioneer family would quickly have met its death in such a hostile environment.

The need for organisation, and for a numerical concentration of settlers, was to be met by the saintly hierarchy of the Mouride brotherhood. The saints first obtained advance knowledge of the precise routes intended for the new railway lines and then moved their disciples to these areas in well-disciplined groups. They provided secure supply lines to the pioneers, most importantly in the overland transport of drinking water. The Fulani were then ousted from the area by diplomatic pressures behind which always lay the threat of force. Where diplomacy and threats went unheeded, the Mourides could mobilise several hundred vigorous young men against a single camp of nomadic Fulani families. Where there was physical struggle (as in the case of Ngonga) the Fulani were inevitably losers, and today they have withdrawn to a safe distance from Mouride farmers. The Mourides today speak willingly enough of the hardships endured by pioneers in confronting the various non-human hazards, but they share with other settlers the comforting view that the land they occupied was 'empty' (i.e. uncultivated) before their arrival. Only the historical records kept by the colonial administration, and the bitter memories of the few Fulani who remain, reveal the extent of violence and intimidation involved in the early phase of settlement. The disemployed Wolof armies (*tyeddo*) who joined the brotherhood in large numbers after 1886, found new employment (and doubtless some pleasure) in clearing the Fulani camps with their massive wooden clubs. The French authorities often turned a blind eye to such events, which they could in any case scarcely control and which did open up new areas to commercial agriculture. Mouride expansion, in some respects a conquest of traditionally Fulani lands by Wolof settlers, thus took on the character of a 'sub-colonisation' within the framework of European rule.

Religious ideology seems to have performed a valuable function for this agrarian colonisation, firstly in the charismatic community which held together a fragile convergence of potentially discordant ambitions: individual saints and disciples recognised a common identity as followers of Amadu Bamba, and differences where they occurred could be arbitrated by the appropriate superior authority within the brotherhood's hierarchy. Ideology also, in the promise of paradise for the loyal disciple, gave an added incentive to work and to endure the hardships of pioneer settlement. 'Non-material incentives', upon which some development economists place so much importance, appear at first glance to have worked in the Mouride case with spectacular success. One might add, finally, that sentiments of 'spiritual' superiority gave an added element of self-righteousness to the settlers, an element which seems very generally important to those engaged in taking other people's land.

The core unit in this pioneering process was the saintly settler camp, or *dara*, a group of some twelve unmarried and landless adult males. These settlers gave their entire harvest to their saintly sponsor, receiving in return only the bare necessities of material subsistence. In the initial phase of colonisation (broadly, pre-1912), when the *daras* were in part a means to escape French authority, the harvest was in the subsistence crop of millet. Later, when the saints had realised the material possibilities offered by collaboration with the French, this was replaced by peanuts – which of course procured cash revenue. The disciples cleared the land and established fields for the wet season, returning to their homelands after the harvest when drought made the wilderness totally uninhabitable.

The disciples' willingness to work in such arduous conditions, and for such meagre immediate reward, suggests a success of 'non-material incentives' of almost insane proportions. But the *dara* situation has proved over time consistently to be temporary and transitional. The disciples, loudly proclaiming their devotion to 'paradise alone', in fact receive their own individual plots of land at the end of some ten years of service.[12] These plots are cut out of the original *dara* estate, which thus eventually disintegrates and is replaced by a village. The saint, to maintain his agrarian power, must find new recruits for *dara* service (easy enough given continued growth of population) and new land to settle. This is a process which still continues at the present time, and which has given the Mourides a bad reputation among agronomists for the practice of shifting cultivation. This reputation, as the above description implies, is on the whole misguided. But the saints now also face increasing difficulty in their search for new land, the western Ferlo itself having become overcrowded. Most of the remaining wilderness area has been 'classified' by the government as a pastoral zone, unsuitable for cultivation in view of the proven fragility of its soil. And it takes a powerful saint, one with good political connections in Dakar, to secure a 'de-classification' of land in this zone: a half dozen of the principal Mouride saints were able to procure allocations of a total of 42,000 acres in their favour in 1962 and 1966. Even the classified zone, if this rate of progress is maintained, will soon disappear, and the saints will then be forced to seek new outlets for their undoubted economic ingenuity.

The pioneer settlers, originally landless, over time have achieved control of their individual holdings. The saintly estate agent has certainly exacted a stiff fee for his services, a rough average of ten years' unremunerated toil in the *dara*. But his disciple clients, it must be remembered, have not been in a strong position to bargain.

PROFANE VILLAGERS

The decisive moment, in the transition from pioneer camp to village, is that when a well is sunk at the site of settlement. A year-round water supply makes permanent habitation possible. The disciple settlers, formally liberated from service by the saint with an assurance of a secured place in heaven, are each awarded their own individual field in the meantime. They then return to their various regions of origin to marry, and return with a wife to set up family on the newly acquired land. The saint, as founder of the village, retains control over the annual distribution of plots of land, but in practice this 'control' becomes a formality as each family cultivates the same plot of land in each succeeding year. The saint nonetheless continues to exact an annual fee for his services in land allocation, as indeed do village chiefs and dignitaries throughout the Wolof zone. This fee is locally given the Muslim designation of *zakāt* (Wolof *assaka*).[13]

In material terms it is significant not only that the settlers are eventually rewarded for their nominally disinterested labours, but also that they are rewarded on the whole equally. Ex-slaves, upon liberation from the saintly settlement, are awarded plots of the same size as freeborn disciples. The saints, in allocating land, apparently have had as principal consideration the ability of each villager to farm his plot with the labour at his disposal. Such a priority has been entirely logical as long as land remained in plentiful supply, although increasing land scarcity is presently making for a more bitter competition among and between villagers (with frequent violent clashes, and queues of wounded at rural medical stations, now an annual routine at sowing time). In any case the history of land settlement until now has been to promote a certain status levelling at least in terms of the traditional Wolof social hierarchy. The only social category to receive significantly smaller land plots has been that of the artisan castes, and this is held to be justified by the fact that artisans devote only a part of their labour time to farming, reserving a proportion for the exercise of their traditional craft.[14] This status levelling in material reality is consolidated (and indeed promoted) by Mouride ideology, which emphasises the equality of disciples before God, Amadu Bamba, and the present-day saints. Class and caste snobbery do indeed persist, but the saints have done much both in material and ideal terms to undermine them – and thereby, clearly, have tended to promote the lower orders of Wolof society (the emergence of *new* forms of social and economic inequality is treated below, in 'Bureaucrats and Co-operators').

Family structure and kinship ties in the new Mouride villages have a characteristic pattern. The basic unit is the compound, a head of family with his wife (or wives) and children, frequently also a younger brother of the family head and less frequently another family dependent or labourer. Land is farmed by the whole compound where the subsistence crop (millet) is concerned, collectively stored and distributed according to need by the compound head. Peanuts are farmed on individual plots by each able-bodied family member (including wives), junior members devoting a proportion of their time to the compound head's fields. The compound head allocates peanut fields within the family, reserving the largest proportion for himself. His position passes upon his death to his eldest son, while the younger brother must himself marry before securing an independent landholding (from vacant land on the village boundary if such remains, from land in a new migrant settlement, or from within the compound itself).

Kinship ties between compounds are as yet infrequent in such villages, the extended family links of each compound tending to be with the particular village and region of origin of the compound head. The saint, in the absence of any elaborate intra-village kinship network (such as is found in long-established villages), is the only focus of social solidarity at the village level. This is not to deny the possibility of mutual economic assistance between villagers, especially in labour at harvest time. But corporate economic activity in the ex-pioneer village is devoted above all to the fields which are set aside for the saint, peanut fields worked by the villagers with the harvest going in entirety to the saint. And it is remarkable, given the saint's centrality to village life and the apparent devotion of his villager disciples, that he in fact receives on average less than one tenth of the villagers' land or labour.[15] Even the present proportion seems to be subject to erosion as the peasants over time tend to lose their sense of gratitude to the village founder and as they experience increasing difficulty in meeting their own material needs (population growth, over-cultivation, soil exhaustion). The saintly fields, which may be seen as a pretext for periodic social gatherings as well as an economic tribute, are a luxury which peasants can less and less afford, and many signs of an increasing reservation on the part of the villager-disciple are now to be remarked in the Mouride zone.

Peasants nonetheless, despite their substantial economic independence, still find the brotherhood's hierarchy useful in dealing with the Senegalese state. This subject is treated in detail below, but in the context of village organisation it is important to remark on the recent growth of village associations (*dā'iras*) which devote a field to the supreme leader of the brotherhood rather than to the local saint. The Khalifa-General of the brotherhood (or indeed his major rival) is sufficiently powerful within the state of Senegal to act effectively as the representative of the economic interests of Mouride peasants, and the growth of associations under his control is in part an indication of a felt need for political guidance and protection in relations with a state bureaucracy which now controls the marketing of the entire peanut harvest in Senegal.

SHANTYTOWN SOCIETIES

Migration of Mouride disciples to the larger towns of Senegal (Dakar, Kaolack, Thiès), and urban settlement on a permanent rather than merely seasonal basis, is a process which has steadily gained momentum since the end of the second world war. The impetus for rural exodus and urban settlement lies essentially in a combination of ecological pressures and positive material inducements, the causal nexus which in earlier years produced massive agrarian colonisation. As new farm land becomes increasingly difficult of access, and as the 'pioneer' zone of the Ferlo fringe now itself suffers from soil exhaustion and overpopulation, the bright lights of the city look increasingly attractive to Mouride disciples. The lights were brighter, admittedly, in the immediate post-war period of economic boom and expanding job opportunities, but even with a post-independence economic recession[16] the marginal possibilities of urban quasi-employment often remain more attractive than the prospect of semi-starvation on the land. By now (1973) there are probably well over 100,000 urban Mourides, and the figures are likely to continue to grow both in absolute terms and as a proportion of the brotherhood's total membership.

Saintly leadership and organisation have as yet adapted only rather tentatively to the recent urbanising drift: the saints themselves preferring in great majority to remain resident in the rural areas where they have securely established power. Urban disciples, thus isolated from their saints, have not abandoned the brotherhood, but they have used their own initiative to develop new forms of organisation adapted to the conditions of urban life. In particular they have created a new form of association in the *dā'ira* (a development of the nineteen-forties, which more recently has spread to the villages). The association is organised by the followers themselves, in general without saintly initiative. It acts to provide mutual aid between disciples, some minimal degree of social security as well as assistance for those seeking employment. It can also function as a kind of trade guild, giving a degree of competitive advantage for example to Mouride tailors, butchers, or petty traders. And finally it provides political organisation for the disciples, and some leverage on municipal and even state authorities. In the bitter struggle for existence which characterises the urban shantytowns, the organised have a substantial advantage over the unorganised. And Mouride urban associations have a special advantage in their continuing links with a very powerful rural organisation. In great majority the associations are directly affiliated to the brotherhood's supreme leader (Khalifa-General) to whom they make an annual offering in cash. This cash tribute, based on regular collections at sessions of religious singing, does not represent a high proportion of the disciples' income (five per cent or less, on average), but it is enough to give some possibility of audience with a leader who in turn has immediate access to the highest authorities in the Senegalese state.

Mouride disciples in the towns nonetheless do also suffer certain handicaps in comparison with other Muslims, most importantly in their relatively poor French language education. The saints in general have been hostile to the state-organised 'French' schools, ostensibly because of Amadu Bamba's persecution at the hands of the colonial authorities, but also because the educated disciple (with job opportunities in the state bureaucracy or the large French-owned companies) tends to become alienated from their authority. There are very few schools in the central Mouride zone (due apparently to saintly influence on the state authorities) and those which do exist are poorly attended (due to saintly influence on disciple parents). Mourides in Dakar were found by the 1955 census to be on average less than half as well educated as other Muslims, Muslims being in turn much less well educated than the Christian minority.[17] Mouride disciples have thus at least initially been confined to occupations not requiring literacy in French, and in immense majority they have become either petty traders or artisans, settling in the poorer shantytown neighbourhoods.

This relatively disadvantaged situation is however at present subject to change, as the urban disciples no longer respond to saintly influence where education is concerned. The material advantages of 'French' education, dubious indeed in reality to a peasant disciple, are starkly evident to anyone engaged in urban job competition. As they become better educated, the disciples are (as the saints rightly feared) also becoming to some degree estranged from the brotherhood. This estrangement has been reinforced by culture contact with other more puritanical Muslims, who deplore the disciples' relative laxity in Islamic observances as well as their apparent subjugation to the saints. Mouride disciples have responded to these contacts by increasing their assiduity in daily prayers, in observing the fast month of Ramadan, and in abstaining from alcoholic liquor. They have, in other words, become 'better Muslims': they have also become worse Mourides.

THE ECONOMICS OF CHARISMA

Each of the three type-situations (pioneer, villager, shanty-towner) involves its own distinct form of economic tribute from disciple to saint, but it should be clear overall that the brotherhood's economic history does not provide supporting evidence for the frequent casual references to Mouride 'feudalism' or 'slavery'. The saints enjoy no rights of land-ownership, merely of temporary and effectively conditional land control, while the element of force or physical constraint is entirely lacking in saintly authority over the disciples. Their control is of course superficially explicable in terms of Mouride ideology, but a review of the three type-situations suggests that economic tribute is in fact roughly proportional to the real material services provided by the saints: agrarian pioneers give the most (ten years of their lives) but also receive the most (a field ultimately wrested from the previous users of the land). It is also true that all disciples are in principle potential beneficiaries of the social security which the brotherhood provides: the saint is nominally obliged, and sometimes effectively acts, to help any disciple who requests a material service. In practice the Mouride welfare state acts perhaps less to serve the old, the sick, the hungry (although these can and do benefit from saintly handouts) than to line the pockets of the holy man's entourage. But the Mourides are not alone among welfare states in tending to redistribute wealth from the poor to the relatively well-off, and even allowing for this tendency there remains a real residual value to the poor in any mechanism which can offer some hope of succour in a very insecure world.

The saints, and especially the brotherhood's principal leaders, have of course done very well for themselves in providing these material and (perhaps) other-worldly services to the disciples. Precise figures for saintly income would be impossible to establish, partly because saints are very discreet on the subject and partly because their characteristically haphazard bookkeeping leaves no reliable record. But it can safely be asserted, when account is made of the various sources of revenue (pioneer estates, village fields, cash tribute) that these incomes are very substantial. The disciples may in general give only a small proportion of their own income, but there are hundreds of thousands of disciples and probably about one hundred major saints. Great saints, whose authority runs in many villages, derive gross incomes of thousands and even tens of thousands of pounds from peanuts alone. The dozen or so saints who act as heads (*Khalīfas*) of important holy lineages (founded by Amadu Bamba's principal collaborators) are the main beneficiaries of this peanut revenue. The supreme head of the brotherhood (Khalifa-General, the founder's heir) also has a substantial income from the urban associations. The saintly elite in general, although most of its income does ultimately come from the disciples' peanut farming, does also derive a substantial revenue in the form of subsidies from the Senegalese state authorities. The great mosque of Touba, apparently the symbol of the disciples' economic devotion, was in large part financed by the colonial administration and by Leopold Senghor's *Union Progressiste Sénégalaise* (which contributed over one hundred thousand pounds to the mosque construction fund for the 1960 election alone). But whatever the source, the major saints undoubtedly do have quite prodigious incomes when seen against the stark agrarian poverty of the great majority of their disciples. Charisma has been a paying proposition.

Saintly charisma or *baraka* (Wolof *barkê*) is thus not altogether surprisingly seen by the disciples above all in material terms. The saints themselves regard their *baraka* as a divine grace which has passed to them from Amadu Bamba, and which helps them in guiding their flock to salvation: in terms of other Sufi brotherhoods, this is an 'orthodox' view. But the disciples, largely illiterate and unconcerned with the convolutions of mystical theology, see *baraka* exclusively in terms of large cars, fine houses, a numerous clientele, and the means by which such good things are acquired – in the words of one disciple, 'wealth above all'. This ignorant and theologically bizarre view of charisma, which seemed to me at first simply an irritating terminological misunderstanding, does not lack its own coherence at the level of empirical sociology. And the disciples do have their own crisp formulation of the process by which charisma has become 'routinised' before their eyes – 'the child of a saint is a king, the child of a king is a thief'. Heaven, for the disciples, is a partially idealised version of the saintly style of life: a plenitude of beautiful concubines, golden hammocks (or at least beds with spring mattresses), lots of tea and sugar and unlimited idle time. In the meantime, the disciples do appear to accept a situation whereby saints can anticipate heaven here on earth, and also to accept (perhaps without undue fervour or conviction) the saint's promise of such an agreeable afterlife for all good and loyal followers.

RELIGIOUS VALUES AND ECONOMIC CHANGE

The characteristic Mouride enthusiasm for agrarian settlement, and for apparently unrewarded labour, have given the disciples a reputation for a peculiar and almost obsessive devotion to hard physical work. At least one scholar (as one might expect) has been led to interpret the brotherhood as yet another exotic variant of Weber's celebrated Protestant Ethic.[18] Other scholars, and many government officials in Senegal, have noted at least a compatibility between Mouride economic ethics and those of the official state programme of economic development. President Senghor himself at a Mouride ceremony in 1963 posed these two apparently rhetorical questions – 'What is Socialism if not, essentially, the socio-economic system which gives priority to work? And who has done this better than Amadu Bamba and his successors?' There is on the face of it some reason to examine the possible empirical basis for an analysis of the brotherhood in such terms. And although the Mourides cannot in the end be very plausibly portrayed either as Muslim Protestants or as Developmental Socialists, a comparative review along these lines may help to bring out some present trends and possible future directions in the continuing economic evolution of the brotherhood.

'Work is a part of religion': this Mouride proverb is only one of a number of exhortations to the disciples to work hard, especially in the service of their saints. A heterodox minority of Mourides even believe that hard labour in the service of a saint can be a substitute for the normal ritual observances of Islam: these are the Bay Fall, led by the descendants of Shaikh Ibra Fall. Most Mourides do observe Islamic obligations (fast, prayer, etc.) albeit with varying rigour, but they do also see work as a valuable complement to these observances. One saint expressed the prevalent official view on a printed card circulated among his followers – 'Devote yourselves to God and to His Prophet, but . . . WORK!!!' (*sic*). The spiritual merit of such work varies to some degree with its character, to a much greater degree with the character of its beneficiary. Agricultural labour, in Tolstoyan fashion, is accorded a particular merit – in the words of one disciple, 'he who works the soil has other benefits beyond his harvest: the work of the soil is the only work that is completely free of sin'. More importantly, the disciple's work *on his own behalf* is of little spiritual significance, while work in the service of a saint is the key to paradise. Statistics gathered in Mouride and other villages demonstrate that the disciples work no harder on average than other peasants in Senegal:[19] there is in fact no generalised Mouride work-ethic, and no reason to be surprised by such statistical evidence. Work is of spiritual value to the disciples only while they serve a saintly aristocracy whose idleness is a concomitant of grace. The clear distinction between working disciple and idle saint also implies the absence of any ascetic element in Mouride belief. Those who conspicuously enjoy their worldly wealth are above all the blessed, whose life of luxury is certainly not seen as evidence of spiritual decay. The perfumed Mouride saint, surrounded by concubines to help pass his idle time, is culturally and otherwise very far removed from Geneva's sombre burghers.

The brotherhood's history of involvement in cash-crop expansion, and the discipline exercised by the saints over their settler disciples, have aroused the interest of a number of agricultural economists. Could the Mourides be 'a force for economic progress'?[20] The saints have certainly helped to open up new lands to cultivation, but they have done so in a manner which if anything makes a negative contribution to prospects of economic development in Senegal. The saint's basic problem has been his need eventually to pay his labour force in land, and therefore to break up his estates and move on after a given period. Aware that his control of the pioneer estate can only be temporary, he has every interest in maximising the immediate cash return.

Trees, which have a long-term value in water-retention and soil preservation, are sacrificed to extend the cultivable area, while fallow periods and crop rotation (with millet) are disregarded in favour of annually repeated peanut cultivation. The disciple settlers, despite their long-run interest in the preservation of land which must eventually devolve to them, are willing in the short run to comply with these practices. The result, on soils which are already fragile and far from ideal for commercial agriculture, is at worst a mining of agrarian resources, the creation in certain localities of something approaching dust-bowl conditions. Mouride villagers, once they leave the saintly settlements, do their best to restore the soil, and (contrary to a prevalent view) are probably no less efficient farmers than most others in Senegal. But the movement of pioneer settlement itself has been accompanied by considerable soil erosion: the Western Ferlo indeed now enjoys a certain notoriety among ecologists as a case where the supply of an infra-structure for agriculture in a pastoral zone has brought about an extension of the desert.

Land is now in any case progressively more scarce even along the desert fringe, and saints in search of new sources of income have of late been directing their attentions increasingly to the towns. Trade, transport, property dealings, these are the characteristic new domains of saintly activity. The preference is for short-term speculation (including money-lending in suitably disguised forms) rather than long-term investment of capital. This is an entirely realistic option given the precarious economic environment of Senegal, but it implies some of the obvious impediments to a development of saintly capitalism on the basis of originally agrarian revenues. The characteristic ethos of capitalism, that disciplined greed which we dignify with the name of rationality, appears for the moment to be beyond the reach of the saints. A taste for luxury goods, a felt need to maintain an extensive (and often expensive) clientele, help to inhibit the impulse to save and re-invest. And in examining the saintly style of life, with all the gratifications of wealth and power, it seems culturally myopic to deny an element of rationality in preferring all this to obsessional saving and carefully-calculated investment. Long-term economic prospects may suggest increasing material problems for the saints, but in the short run life is good and in the long run there is always paradise.

The disciples also would be very reserved about any role which the saints might wish to allocate them in an urban capitalism, unless that role were demonstrably to their own advantage. The eminence of the saints today owes much to the manner in which they have provided organisational focus to a highly effective community response to the impact of capitalism on Wolof society. The ethic of Mouride solidarity certainly helped to contain the potentially destructive intrusion of the market economy. The disciples are well aware of the material services which the saints have provided, especially in providing access to new land. Land remains the key to the Mouride success story: the brothers cannot convincingly be portrayed as slaves, serfs, or indeed as 'factors of progress'. The disciples over the years have been in a position to do their own unarticulated cost-benefit analysis of saintly leadership, and the balance up to now appears on the whole positive. Beneath all the spectacular ritual of subjection, and allowing for a real price in temporary deprivation, this has been one occasion when the meek really did inherit the earth.

NOTES

1 P. Marty, *Les Mourides d'Amadou Bamba*, Paris: Leroux, 1913. The most important subsequent studies conducted under the auspices of the colonial administration are the unpublished report of L. Nekkach, 'Le Mouridisme Depuis 1912', completed in 1952 (available in the Dakar Archives) and the published reports collected in *Centre de Hautes Etudes Administratives sur l'Afrique et l'Asie Modernes* (ed.), *Notes et Etudes sur l'Islam en Afrique Noire*, Paris: Peyronnet, 1962.
2 Afrique Occidentale Française, Territoire du Sénégal, *Aménagement de l'Economie Agricole et Rurale du Sénégal*, Dakar, 1952 (Mission R. Portères), p. 108.
3 L. C. Behrman, *Muslim Brotherhoods and Politics in Senegal*, Cambridge Mass.: Harvard University Press, 1970, p. 104.
4 C. T. Sy, *La Confrérie Sénégalaise des Mourides*, Paris: Présence Africaine, 1969. V. Monteil, 'Une Confrérie Musulmane: les Mourides du Sénégal', in *Archives de Sociologie des Religions*, No. 14, 1962.
5 A paper delivered to a Paris conference in 1968, subsequently published in *Cahiers d'Etudes Africaines (C.E.A.)*, outlines my initial reaction to the research experience. D. Cruise O'Brien, 'Le talibé mouride', in *C.E.A.* No. 35, 1969 and *C.E.A.* No. 40, 1970.
6 J. Copans *et al.*, *Maintenance Sociale et Changement Economique au Sénégal*, Vol. I, *Doctrine Economique et Pratique du Travail chez les Mourides*, Paris: O.R.S.T.O.M., 1972. This volume, co-authored by J. Copans, P. Couty, J. Roch and G. Rocheteau, includes case studies on four Mouride villages, with precise figures for the labour time and landholdings of a sample of families.
7 D. Cruise O'Brien, *The Mourides of Senegal*, Oxford: Clarendon Press, 1971. This work, a revised form of my doctoral thesis, contains most of the detailed evidence for the argument made here.
8 Only a degree of culture shock can excuse my slowness in perceiving the full implications of this remark, later repeated on a number of similar occasions.
9 The term ideology here refers to the more or less integrated set of beliefs shared by members of the brotherhood. The Mouride case accords quite closely with Mannheim's definition of ideology as a 'more or less conscious disguise of the real nature of a situation', the true recognition of which is not in the interests of members of the group in question. K. Mannheim, *Ideology and Utopia* (Gerth and Shils trans.), New York: Harcourt Brace, 1964 (first published 1936), p. 55.

10 For examples, see D. Cruise O'Brien, *The Mourides*. . . pp. 222, 233–4, 277–8.
11 Dates are important here. The first line to be completed was that from Dakar to St Louis (across Kayor) in 1885. A line from Thiès across eastern Senegal was begun in 1907, and completed at Kayes in 1923 (this ran across the region of Saloum). Two further lines were completed in 1931, one in the region of Jolof (Louga-Linguère) and one in Baol (Diourbel-Touba, with free unskilled labour supplied by the Mourides).
12 The extent to which this has been the case was originally underestimated by me (see *The Mourides*. . . , p. 174) but it does emerge from a detailed examination of the land settlement pattern as a historical process in particular villages or indeed in general.
13 Such fees have nominally been suppressed by the Senegalese state under the Law on the National Domain of 1964, which legally recognises the right of each peasant to the land he cultivates. State law in this case has yet to have much impact on local rural practices.
14 For statistics and detail on Wolof class and caste in landholding, see J. Copans *et al*., notably pp. 100 (Couty), 142 (Roch), 168 (Copans).
15 *Ibid*. pp. 148, 183, 212, 252 and throughout.
16 The economic crisis following independence was particularly acute for Senegal (and Dakar industry in particular) with the break-up of the Federation of French West Africa. The loss of Dakar's status as federal capital, and the narrowing of industrial markets, contributed to the recession.
17 Afrique Occidentale Française, Haut Commisariat de la République, *Recensement Démographique de Dakar* (1955), Premier Fascicule, Paris, July 1958, p. 83.
18 A. Wade, 'La Doctrine Economique du Mouridisme', Dakar, 1966 (roneo).
19 J. Copans *et al*., pp. 150–1, 251 and throughout.
20 See R. Dumont, *L'Afrique Noire est mal Partie*, Paris: Seuil, 1962, p. 120, and République du Sénégal, *Rapport Général sur les Perspectives de Développement du Sénégal*, Dakar, CINAM, 1960, Vol. I, Ch. 1–5.

3

CHIEFS, SAINTS AND BUREAUCRATS

CHIEFS, SAINTS AND BUREAUCRATS

Dynamics of power and authority under colonial rule

Technical superiority in the means of violence, in military equipment and organisation, made possible the gradual extension of French control over the hinterland of Senegal in the late nineteenth century (1852–1900). The motive drive behind this imperial expansion, a combination of simple economic greed (market outlets, resources) and a more diffuse yearning for national glory, lies beyond the concern of this study: but it may be noted that the opportunity went some way to contribute its own motive. The local French military officers, whose victories left their metropolitan superiors with ever-expanding (and not always entirely welcome) territorial responsibilities, had their own belligerent impulses – and the means to make such impulses effective. Those Africans who attempted armed resistance, in the Wolof zone (or elsewhere) succeeded only in demonstrating the brave futility of their stand.

General acknowledgment (by 1900) of these harsh military facts provided the secure basis for colonial peace, making possible first the acceptance of French government and then a general compliance with the conqueror's economic exactions. A dominant culture and mode of political and economic organisation were thus forcibly imposed upon an agglomeration of subordinated societies now contained within the arbitrarily drawn boundaries of the new colonial territory of Senegal. Questions of sociological legitimacy at first sight seem irrelevant to the survival of such a system.

Yet these stark outlines of the violence underlying the colonial situation can also be deceptive on closer examination, and they certainly do not lead very far in analysing the workings of the political system of colonial rule in Senegal. The enforced dominance of an alien minority in this situation had quite intricate and contradictory results – certainly not reducible to a simple racial subjection of black to white. Conquest and enforced submission, including slavery, were after all already facts of life in the Senegal area long before French military intrusion in the interior. French conquest was not the disruption of an African Garden of Eden, it was new not in its oppressiveness but in the quality of economic and political organisation which it introduced. And there were to be many Africans (and more specifically in this context, Wolof) who found reasons to welcome at least some of the conqueror's innovations.

From the conqueror's standpoint, the legacy of efficient violence was an elementary political problem – given a tight colonial budget, and given limited local French personnel, how to make an administration effective? The objectives of administration might also be limited enough – to keep the peace, to collect taxes, and where possible to ensure the establishment of remunerative forms of agriculture – but the problem was compounded by the stubborn facts of cultural distance between coloniser and colonised (especially in the rural areas, where very little French is spoken to this day). And neither (latent) violence nor high policy directives proved to be of much assistance to the local French colonial officer in discharging the day-to-day duties which the situation of conquest had left him.

Official French colonial policy, as defined at the highest ministerial levels in Paris, and as stated in the broadest terms, hinged on the debate between the tendencies labelled as 'Assimilation' and on the other hand 'Association'.[1] The assimilation of Africans to French culture (*civilisation*) was never seen as other than a very long term objective, and in application never reached beyond a small educated and urbanised elite (although it certainly proved effective enough among the Wolof '*évolués*' of Dakar and St Louis). Association as a policy principle indicated little more than a vaguely defined paternal tutelage, *not* involving the impractical and probably undesirable mass conversion of Africans into Frenchmen. Such a debate in effect reflected little more than the competing ideological preferences of the rival metropolitan political parties. For practical administrative purposes, it was paper-consuming phoney.

At the next level of the French official hierarchy, the West African federal administration in Dakar, these dubious ideological polarities (assimilation/association) were little discussed or doubtless even considered. Here more practical considerations began to intrude – most specifically, given the paucity of French personnel, *which* Africans to use in building a viable administrative structure? And the dominant tendency was first and most clearly defined by Governor General William Ponty (1909–15), a *politique des races* whereby French authority should work through approved native chiefs, such chiefs being recruited from the tribes which they would administer after a training course in French administrative principles.[2] An important objective of this policy was to preserve non-Muslim tribes from the dangerous contagion of Islam, and to avoid the mistakes of an earlier period in which Islam had been inadvertently encouraged by the use of Muslim intermediaries to enforce French authority even where the intermediaries were not of the given local tribe. France should so far as possible rely on secular (or secularised) intermediaries: in the terms of this argument, the preference was for chiefs rather than saints.

A contrary tendency however always existed, with more than a foothold in the offices of the Governor General at

Dakar. The relevant precedent here was that of French policy in Algeria, as first mediated (1854–65) by Governor Faidherbe and later by a remarkable group of French Islamist scholar-administrators whose activities were to centre around the *Service des Affaires Musulmanes* at Dakar (founded 1906). The leading figures of this group were Paul Marty, author of a series of thoroughly documented studies on Islam in France's various West African colonies; Robert Arnaud (known also as the colonial novelist Robert Randau), author of a study of Mauritania as well as a very persuasive and well-reasoned general statement of France's 'Islamic policy'; and the most eminent among these already exceptional scholars, Xavier Coppolani, co-author of a thorough study of North African Muslim brotherhoods, well-known at least in colonial circles for the colourful circumstances of his death – stabbed in a tent by a Muslim fanatic while engaged on an exploratory mission in Mauritania. Each of these colonial scholars, reflecting back on the successes enjoyed in Algeria, favoured (albeit with various reservations and qualifications) France's administrative co-option of the saints of the West African Muslim brotherhoods.[3]

Muslim notables could at the least be valuable informal intermediaries in dealing with tribes such as the Wolof, where Islam was a securely (and apparently irrevocably) established religion. Behind this administrative preference lay something more than the obvious considerations of expediency, a French *laïc* inclination to annoy the (Catholic) priests. Emile Combes, while in power in Paris (1902–5) even apparently carried his secularist revivalism far enough to propose the establishment of Islam as an official state religion in France's colonies.[4] Catholic missionaries in West Africa throughout the colonial period complained of the pro-Islamic preferences of senior administrators, with a stream of dark hints at the power of freemasons in high places.[5] Where the Wolof were concerned, the Combes project was put into effect at least on an informal basis, not perhaps as a duly deliberated policy. But the 'pro-Islamic' orientation did receive some official recognition. In 1906 for example the 'School for the Sons of Chiefs' at St Louis (the academy for training official colonial chiefs) took the name of a Franco-Muslim *Médersa* (giving one third of its curriculum to training in Islam). And the saints, if not French functionaries, were showered with French medals and decorations.

Official recognition of Islam, however it may have been conceived by the senior colonial officers of Paris and Dakar, above all responded to immediate problems of local administration where Muslim subjects (such as the Wolof) were concerned. With few French officials, not more than a dozen for some half a million rural Wolof, and a rapid turnover (*rouage*) of colonial staff, there was effectively very little choice in the matter. The local French colonial officer could draw little useful guidance from the vague proclamations of his administrative superiors. Short of money, short of staff, he also had the expediencies of his own career to consider. These career considerations effectively placed important restrictions on the actual use of France's superior technology of violence. A colonial officer, if he allowed a local situation to deteriorate so far as to necessitate an assertion of force, incurred the displeasure of his superiors. He had been clumsy, and he had incurred expense: no ticket for promotion there. The local French officer thus did well to cultivate his associations with influential African subjects who could assure peaceful compliance in the collection of taxes and the provision of recruits for military or labour service.

In the Wolof zone, as elsewhere in Senegal, expediency suggested a preference for saints rather than chiefs. The chiefs enjoyed little local popularity, partly in memory of their pre-colonial oppression and partly for reasons developed below. The saints were not only popular, as again argued below, but they also adhered to a religion which was known, written down, and even translated into French: the cultural gap between ruler and subject might not readily be bridged, but it could at least be codified. The local French official had no need (even in the unlikely event of his having the desire or the possibility) to be an amateur anthropologist, no need to know anything of the vestigial pre-Islamic Wolof culture and social structure. When confronted by a local dispute, he had only to consult his indexed Seignette translation of Sidi Khalil (cheap too at 25 francs).[6] There might be no surer method of eradicating pagan survivals, but equally one can readily see the advantages of this procedure for the harassed administrator beset by incomprehensible African claimants. Pre-Muslim Wolof tradition was only invoked by the French in altogether exceptional circumstances, and to eliminate particularly troublesome individuals. Otherwise pagan tradition was quite simply impractical for administration, providing no written rules: such, for the saints, were the uses of literacy.

To whatever extent French 'policy' remained a matter of day-to-day expediency, and despite the coercion always at least latent in the colonial situation, in practice also the colonial rulers could not quite disregard the question of a *legitimate* authority. And although the French had brought (enforced) peace to the Wolof, and a relative material prosperity, they remained culturally alien and unable to command more than a distant gratitude even from those subjects who had gained most from colonial rule. Legitimate authority remained the prerogative of the Muslim saints, and the French were in effect obliged to accept a second-hand legitimacy through the saints whom they used. This acceptance gives an ironical twist to a French view of Islam as a step up on the ladder to civilisation (French) from the depths of pagan barbarism: Islam, in other words, as an indirect (or second-hand) variant of Assimilation.[7] Legitimacy or Assimilation at second hand may be no more than two views of the same process. But from whatever perspective, an understanding of the process demands closer consideration of the agents at first hand, the African mediators. And here it rapidly becomes apparent that colonial rule had created a *political* situation in which there was very much more room for African initiative than administrative appearances might at first sight suggest.

The formal structures of colonial administration did in part define, but also concealed, the workings of this political situation. The subjects, even in the rural areas which are the main concern of this essay, were to be no undifferentiated mass of helpless victims. Some had the skill or good fortune to benefit very substantially from the French presence. This is very evident in the case of those Africans who occupied administrative roles within the colonial state, but there are also many cases in which whole groups or social categories were able to win for themselves very substantial new resources within the framework of colonial rule. French conquest in Senegal was of course accompanied by the imposition not only of new administrative structures, but also of a new economic system, fundamentally involving the cultivation of peanuts for export by the local peasantry. Commercialisation in the rural sector (especially developed in the Wolof region) was accompanied by rapid social change – demographic expansion, urbanisation, the disruption of kinship based groups by market competition, and the differentiation of individuals and groups on the basis of their economic success in the new system ('Bureaucrats and Co-operators', below). These changes were in large part *effected* by colonial rule, but the point to be emphasised here is that they were not closely *controlled* within the colonial system. The reach of colonialism (its economic and social impact) may be said to have exceeded its grasp (its ability – or desire – to manage the political consequences).

The political latitude enjoyed by African intermediaries has been stressed in studies of 'administrative' chieftaincies in other colonies – especially in situations where the European government employed a policy of 'indirect rule' in controlling its African subjects.[8] The case of Senegal would suggest that a policy of 'direct rule' could in practice involve rather similar political consequences. The rural African agents of colonial authority were later to be denounced by (urban) nationalist politicians as 'stooges' or 'tools' of the colonialists, but their role was characteristically more ambivalent. The label 'tool' is best restricted to inanimate objects, and even stooges must calculate and defend their own political interests if they are to survive.

Nor do individual machinations on the part of such intermediaries by any means exhaust the possibilities of political action for the colonial subjects. There were also the communal struggles which were reshaped under European rule, in which for example certain tribal groups could win decisive local advantages against others by securing the confidence of the French: such was the case of the Mandinka tribe in the Casamance region, which extended its zone of commercial and political influence to areas inhabited by previously hostile tribes.[9] Or again, in which Muslims in general could come to dominate local pagans on the basis of the cultural superiority which many administrators ascribed to Islam. These communal struggles could even begin to assume a class character as new bases of social differentiation began to overlay the old, with economic success in the field of commercial agriculture, notably, or favourable geographic location close to a major urban development.

Remarks such as the above, with certain modifications, apply no doubt fairly widely in African colonial situations, at least in areas without white settlement. African intermediaries under the colonial regime were thus involved in a rapidly changing social situation, in which there were real political (and economic) opportunities for those who could identify the direction of change and who could use their initiative to turn it to advantage. The purpose of this argument is to examine certain of the means to which this initiative might have been employed among the Wolof. The period chosen is that from the completion of military conquest (late 1880s) to the year 1945 – which opens a new period when 'democratisation' and political reform in the colonies began to modify the authoritarian structure of French administration.

Three crucial roles are here identified among the very many types of African intermediary, and are analysed in their relationship to French authority, to the African subjects, and to each other. The first of these is that of the *chief*, the Wolof ruler whose position was based on hereditary eligibility to office and also to some extent on political talent; the second is the Muslim *saint*, who emerged as the charismatically designated representative of rural society in crisis; the third, the *bureaucrat*, is the subordinate official nominated by colonial superiors. The selection of these three types may be taken to suggest an application of Weber's typology of legitimate authority (traditional, charismatic, rational-legal). There is indeed a sense in which this is the case, although the central concern here is with the working out of these roles in relation to an external authority. The argument is thus concerned with the distribution of power in a colonial political system, and with the styles in which African power was exercised. These styles are seen to evolve over time, in response to the changes introduced by the French authorities: thus it is argued that the traditional chiefs under colonial rule became deviant bureaucrats, while the Muslim saints tended increasingly to assume the functions and political style of the previous chiefs.

CHIEFS AND BUREAUCRATS

The position of the Wolof chief in the period prior to French conquest had increasingly become that of a military leader, whose eligibility to office was determined by a combination of matrilineal and patrilineal descent, but whose power largely rested on the group of armed retainers (*tyeddo*) which he maintained. Military defeat at the hands of the French was disastrous to this system of chiefly power. As a warrior leader, whose right to rule had come to depend on the conspicuous display of authority and strength, the chief suffered very fundamentally from the humiliation of defeat in battle and of incorporation into an administrative hierarchy in which he became the white man's subordinate agent. His soldiers were disarmed and dismissed, his states were rapidly broken up into the smaller standard *canton* units, and his functions were reduced by a series of administrative decrees: his legal powers of authoritative arbitration and punishment were taken over by courts under French officials (decrees of 1903, 1912, 1924), while his economic power in the allocation of individual rights to cultivate the land was simply abolished (decree of 1906).[10] The French colonial administration was designed as a bureaucratic hierarchy, of military inspiration, in which the upper levels of officialdom (the commissioned officers) were exclusively of French origin – the Governor General of French West Africa, Governor of Senegal, *Commandant de Cercle*, *Chef de Subdivision*. Beneath this European hierarchy were the 'African levels' of officialdom, in rural society some ten official grades, but essentially the canton and village chiefs – sergeants and corporals respectively. The position of the canton chief, at the highest standard level of African command,[11] was crucial: the French colonial system made this administrative position at least formally a bureaucratic one in almost all important respects.

(a) *Specification of functions*: the chief's functions were rapidly reduced to those of tax collection, military recruitment, and the provision of compulsory labour for various tasks. In conjunction with the village chiefs, he should help to provide the basic census data to be used in these various levies. In discharging all these tasks, he should proceed according to fixed rules established by superior officers.

(b) *Hierarchy*: policy decisions were taken at the European levels of authority, and carried out where necessary by the chiefs. Appointment or dismissal of chiefs rested (from 1887 in Senegal) exclusively with French authority. 'Traditional' status or eligibility to office was given some weight, but was never more than one of a number of relevant considerations, of which perhaps the most important was the candidate's known submissiveness to French authority (ex-servants of French officials, or veterans of the French army, were frequently appointed on the basis of this last qualification).

(c) *Specialised training*: candidates for canton chieftaincies were educated (increasingly over time) at the School for the Sons of Chiefs (*Médersa*) at St Louis, where they took a four year course in administration and related fields. Upon graduation, they were liable to eighteen months' military service, before being posted as clerk or interpreter to a French local official pending a vacancy in a chieftainship.

(d) *Administration based on documents and files*: the literate chief was expected to maintain written records which could be scrutinised by his superiors.

(e) *Full-time employment*: the job of canton chief was a full-time one, but the mode of remuneration diverged from bureaucratic procedure. The chief was indeed paid a fixed annual salary, but he was *also* paid with a fixed proportion of the taxes which he raised – a prebendary form of payment which opened the way to a wide variety of non-bureaucratic procedures.

The *administrative* position of the canton chief was in most respects a bureaucratic one, accepting Weber's criteria for a bureaucratic system.[12] Yet the *political* position of these officials is scarcely intelligible in such terms. The formal bureaucratic apparatus was also in reality a two caste hierarchy, in which a small white ruling caste (of limited resources in finance and personnel) made use of numerous agents from the subject population to maintain control. The canton chief stood at the cultural and political boundary between ruler and ruled, and his position as privileged intermediary could be used to establish considerable independent authority. His political role bears comparison with that of the rural Indian 'middleman' in electoral politics, as analysed by F. G. Bailey, a Kafkaesque messenger between the village and the wider world: 'suspicion of deviousness, if not deceitful activity, is inherent in the middleman's role, for while it exists to make communications between opponents, its strength depends upon keeping these communications imperfect'.[13] The chief handled the demands of the ruling group, essentially for 'blood, sweat and taxes' (Lasswell) which he could often 'interpret' to considerable personal or factional advantage. Taxation, military recruitment, forced labour levies – even the provision of census data – all provided occasions on which friends and dependents could be leniently treated while enemies and others could make good the balance. A canton chief of the post-1945 period of electoral politics gave some indication of such possibilities when he warned his opponents – 'woe to those who vote for the *Bloc Democratique Sénégalais*, my tax census will be implacable for them'.[14] A chief could use his discretion in providing prestation labour to the French authorities, so that his clients would be untouched, while opponents could be chosen on several consecutive occasions.

Local factional struggles were fought out in this manner, while the French administration remained above all concerned with the overall success of the chief in meeting the demands made upon him. The chief's political autonomy could be maintained the more effectively where he could also control the flow of reactions from the subjects to the ruler. Where he could place a clientele among the local French official's African guard, for example, it would be difficult to secure direct access to make complaints against chiefly abuses.[15] French officials, in general almost entirely ignorant of local language and customs, often made it possible for the chief to turn this ignorance to advantage. A case from the Cameroons, cited by R. L. Buell, gives an eloquent, burlesque suggestion of the possibilities of political manipulation at the cultural boundary:

> . . . a native came with a grievance against his chief to a local (French) officer, who told him to take his hat off. The interpreter, who was apparently under the control of the chief concerned, told the native that 'white man would cut his palaver tomorrow'. The native thereupon remonstrated with the French official who again repeated, 'Take your hat off!' The interpreter thereupon told the native that 'the white man says to get out of the office'.[16]

Popular memory among the Wolof would credit their chiefs with such intrigues in abundance. French colonial officials could not (or would not) keep too close an eye on their subordinates. At the local level they were often reluctant to embark on fatiguing tours of supervision in their districts as long as the chief seemed to keep control. Some French officials were suspicious of chiefs in general, or even hostile to them, but many seem to have taken the view that any tendency to discredit the chiefs should be checked since it brought their own authority into question.[17]

Factors such as these made it effectively impossible to implement the official policy of establishing 'direct' French control over the subject population: an official source was later to note that 'while indirect administration failed, direct administration was no more successful . . . above all because the basic instrument of European administrative systems – writing – was lacking among the subjects'[18] (true of course especially of non-Muslims). The canton chiefs, in these circumstances, remained political animals in bureaucratic clothing. Yet the extent of the chief's latitude as intermediary was limited, and his 'autonomous' power tended to exacerbate the exploitationary character of the colonial system. If a chief could raise 'unofficial' taxes or labour recruits in excess of the official quota, and could use this revenue and work force to enrich himself and maintain a clientele, he could only do so while continuing to meet all the demands placed upon him by French superiors. Only a small minority could be exempt, an entourage of clients who often gave valuable assistance to the chief in discharging his functions, while the rest suffered in varying degrees. Failure to supply the French with their official quota led to dismissal, and dismissal meant instant loss of revenue and power: very few chiefs had any significant independent economic resources. Some chiefs were able to build up a landholding while in office, but very few could retain the land when their official position had been lost.[19]

The canton chief's relation to his subjects was in any case clearly remote from that of the ideal typical neutral bureaucrat. He was a sub-tyrant whose excesses could only be curbed by the occasional intervention of superior tyrants. His power within a narrowly defined sphere was great, but the basis of his former legitimacy had disappeared as he no longer performed any function valued by the mass of his subjects. These subjects, although oppressed, were not wholly without political resources, and their reactions indeed have done much to shape the political history of Senegal. They began for example to seek more direct access to European officials, by-passing the chiefs, through African 'letter-writers' who could make complaints in the proper form and through appropriate channels. A schoolteacher in the neighbouring French colony of Mali in the 1930s recalled his role in this regard: 'There are different ways of playing politics. At that time to make a verbal or written intervention in favour of a friend or relative (or any other person who seemed to be wronged) was to play politics. To signal in high places certain irregularities committed by the chiefs of villages or of cantons, by officials supported by the *Commandant de Cercle*, this also was to play politics.'[20] One might add that possibilities for blackmail also developed in these situations, and could be lucrative for literate Africans with detailed knowledge of local 'irregularities'. 'Letter-writers' were an important constituent element in the Senegalese political elite which was to come into its own after 1945 ('Clans, clienteles and communities', below). Above all, however, the subjects in the Wolof zone reacted to chiefly oppression by turning to the already established leadership group provided by the local Islamic brotherhoods.

SAINTS AND CHIEFS

The pre-colonial crisis of the Wolof states, already described in some detail, is vividly summarised in this (frequently quoted) passage by the French Islamist Robert Arnaud:

> In Wolof country, formerly, the intrusion of Islam constituted a true social revolution, and was in reality an opposition of the proletariat to the aristocracy, a class struggle. The cultivators had a violent dislike for the warriors, who exploited them. Thanks to

Islam they formed a solid block against the still fetishist aristocracy, and the *Marabouts* were for a long time the natural leaders of the crowd against its oppressors.[21]

French conquest had halted the armed struggle of these rival parties, but it also sharply accentuated the social crisis which that struggle had initiated. The effect of this crisis was to turn the entire Wolof people to Muslim leadership. Three Muslim brotherhoods,[22] the Mourides and the older established Qãdiriyya and Tijãniyya, came to control the spiritual allegiances of the Wolof people. The hierarchy of religious grace (*baraka*) within the brotherhoods, in which authority was justified by patrilineal descent from saintly ancestors, thus became a parallel hierarchy of political authority outside the framework of alien rule.

Colonialism was of course among other things a clash of values and ideologies, and it does appear that Islam also provided an effective means of cultural defence at a time when Wolof culture and localised 'pagan' beliefs could no longer do so. The functions of Islam as a political ideology have been noted in other colonial situations: and as Clifford Geertz remarks of Morocco and Indonesia, the Muslim religion established a secure cultural line between coloniser and colonised – 'colonialism created the conditions in which an oppositional, identity preserving, willed Islam could and did flourish . . .'.[23] This was clearly enough the case in Senegal in the period immediately following French conquest. While holy war against the French had to be rejected as a doomed enterprise, the Muslim leaders who acquired the largest followings were often those who took their distance from the conqueror and refused to collaborate. Despite such veiled opposition, it also remained the case that Islam was a religion which the conqueror on the whole respected.

The saints of the Muslim brotherhoods, with their clienteles of religious disciples, were not incorporated into the hierarchy of French officialdom. As the chiefs were deprived of their previous functions by French decrees, and as the French had no alternative administrative structures for the effective discharge of many of these functions, they tended to devolve to Muslim leadership. Again, and for comparison with the chiefly bureaucrat dealt with above, it may be useful to itemise some of the principal features of the role of the saintly chief.

(a) *Functions*: there were of course the traditional functions of the religious guide – teacher, prayer leader, healer, magician, redeemer. To these were added several which the chiefs had been forced to abandon: legal arbitration (albeit informal), the annual distribution of plots of land among cultivators, and the provision of a minimal form of social security for the aged and sick. In the transition to a generalised cash crop economy, finally, the Muslim leaders provided many useful services – relatively cheap credit, stocking of food against periodic price falls and crop failures, transport and marketing facilities, being some of the more important. The better organised Muslims (notably the Mourides) of course also took advantage of the possibilities created by the extension of railway lines across the interior, opening up new lands to migration and commercial cultivation.

(b) *Appointment*: the great Muslim leaders of the preconquest and conquest period owed their position to the qualities their followers recognised in them. These were leadership qualities of a broadly charismatic type, and the popular response may be seen against the background of profound social crisis described above. In the colonial period, the 'routinisation' of this leadership meant that accession to office depended effectively on spiritual (and genealogical) inheritance from a saintly ancestor, although popular recognition of this legitimacy still to some degree depended on the skill of particular heirs.[24] Appointment by a combination of skill and heredity was of course very much the mode of the preconquest chiefs, and the Muslim leaders avoided the subsequent fate of the chiefs in that they did not owe their place to nomination by colonial superiors (with a few notable exceptions).

(c) *Hierarchy*: the organisational structure of the religious brotherhoods provided for a hierarchy of spiritual authority, formalised in rituals of initiation and submission. The political effectiveness of these hierarchies varied greatly from case to case, but in general they allowed at least a fairly effective co-ordination of action in particular lodges or local clusters, and they provided a basis for the relatively orderly allocation of geographical spheres of spiritual-political influence.

(d) *Remuneration*: the revenues of the Muslim leaders were drawn from the voluntary labour of the disciples on their peanut estates, and from pious 'gifts' (often, as already suggested, a form of tribute in return for the right to cultivate). Agricultural labour and cultivation fees had been among the principal sources of chiefly income in the past, but the Muslim leaders with the expansion of commercial agriculture were in a position to make them very much more remunerative.

The abundant new revenue of the saints had many political uses. It could be used to purchase the support or collusion of administrative chiefs, as one French official noted in 1913 when he deplored the saints' ability 'all too frequently . . . to corrupt our native entourage'.[25] It could be used to subsidise the electoral campaigns of the Senegalese politicians of the Four Communes, who would intervene on the Muslim leaders' behalf in St Louis, Dakar, or Paris. It could even be used on occasion across cultural and political boundaries to compromise or corrupt local

French administrative officials – some of whom were glad enough, it seems, to augment their meagre salaries in this way. The Senegalese commune politician, Galandou Diouf, remarked on this privately on more than one occasion, and a hint to the same effect can be found in an editorial in a local newspaper of 1926.[26] A discreet use of the surplus gained from commercial agriculture enabled the Muslim leaders to secure a degree of immunity from administrative exactions, and also to secure administrative recognition of their right to large areas of land.

The saints were inevitably themselves used by the French in many ways; in periodic campaigns to increase local agricultural production, for example, or in recruitment for the armed forces. Unlike the chiefs, however, they were in a position to exact a price for their collaboration in such enterprises, and often to use these occasions to increase their own power and prestige. Their assistance was *solicited* by the French, not (as in the case of the chiefs) obtained by peremptory order. A French official in 1945 remarked that the saints had much enlarged their clienteles as a result of the public favour shown to them by the colonial administration, and that their collaboration with the French had done more to further their own ends than it had for the 'general interest' (*sic*).[27]

Thus the Wolof chiefs found that colonial rule had accomplished the victory which the saints had initially been denied by French conquest. Some chiefs in the early period of colonial rule tried to use their administrative status to take measures against Muslim opponents, but the balance of power shifted rapidly against them as they lost prestige and popular following. The chiefs then progressively came to submit themselves to Muslim authority; some became courtiers in a religious entourage, a few became holy men themselves, many became mere disciples.

The social position of the saints was of course transformed by these trends under colonial rule. At a village level the chief in the Wolof area was overshadowed by the local Muslim notable(s). The village chief indeed often became a 'straw chief' who was responsible for the various French exactions, while local leadership in every other sphere fell to the men of religion. At the canton level the chiefs had more extensive arbitrary power, but the Muslim leaders could exert influence over them both by positive incentives (bribes, or promises to intercede with the French for their advancement) and by threats to discredit them in French eyes.

The contrasting effects of French rule on chiefly and saintly power are nowhere better illustrated than in the drive for support of France's military efforts undertaken during the first and second world wars. In these exceptional circumstances the exploitationary character of the colonial system was most accentuated. The chiefs then raised recruits for the forces, and increased local agricultural production, only by means of coercion (fines, forced labour, arbitrary imprisonment, seizure of 'volunteers') which prepared their own downfall after 1945: a French administrator remarked of the first world war as 'the time when we took volunteers by lasso'.[28] The saints, who at first often helped their followers to escape the military recruitment drives, were able then (informally) to negotiate terms for their support – access to uncultivated land, freedom from administrative harassment, almost a *Combiste* recognition of Islam as Senegal's state religion. The disciples who went to fight for France could be offered an inducement – a small plot of new land if they returned, a guaranteed place in paradise if they did not. Thus the Muslim leaders emerged from the second world war not only with French confidence but with an increased popular following, while the chiefs were more hated than ever.

CONCLUSION

A poorly financed colonial administration, with its very small core of French officials and restricted objectives, had been charged with the supervision of a social situation which evolved with bewildering rapidity. And it is thus scarcely surprising that Wolof intermediaries were in a position to draw considerable personal or even group advantage from the inability of the French to control the situation without their help. For the preceding argument, this is most evident in the case of the Muslim saints, where the French effectively bypassed their own official bureaucratic structures in favour of an informal version of British 'indirect rule'.

The reaction of the subjects to the latent violence of the colonial situation, in these circumstances, was a complex one. Colonial rule had brought internal peace to a society in which warfare had become endemic, with an immediate and marked increase in the material well-being of the mass of cash cropping farmers. (The long-run effects, with demographic expansion and market stagnation, being less positive – 'Co-operators and bureaucrats' below.) The elimination of the Wolof warrior aristocracy (*tyeddo*) permitted something like a democratic upsurge of the lower class dependents, who turned to the Muslim saints. Many Wolof thus had good reason to welcome the French, and the copious expressions of popular gratitude in the period following the conquest cannot be taken to have been merely complaisant. Racial hostility to whites has always been fairly muted in Wolof society, and even the paternalist visions of colonial administrators were not without an element of truth.

Popular hostility to the French conquerors did nonetheless persist beneath the surface of political life, even among those groups who had gained most substantially from the colonial peace. The paternalist vision of the grateful subject is perhaps always misleading: no trusteeship, even if benevolent, can heal the wounded self-respect of a people condemned to perpetual dependence. Islam had helped to conserve self-respect, permitting at least a cultural distance from the conqueror, and in certain cases a fine contempt for the alien non-believers (Nazarenes). This undercurrent of popular hostility to the French was thus an important factor in the triumph of Muslim leadership in the post-conquest period. Yet it was also, in the long run, a potential threat to the position of that leadership.

As the saint became an instrument of colonial indirect rule, he could conserve his authority only by playing on the ambiguities of his intermediary role – 'pretending to be a policeman in such a way that everyone would recognise them for a thief', as Bailey remarks of his Indian middleman.[29] This is of course a very difficult game to play, and one can only admire the skill with which it often was played. Over time, nonetheless, this form of intermediary role can scarcely fail to be affected by the intermediary's awareness (and fear) of the ultimate arbitrary power of the dominant alien minority. Thus the saints, by the end of the period under consideration (1880–1945) had moved appreciably closer to the position of the subordinated chiefs as agents of European authority – always present to celebrate the 14th of July, protesting loyalty as their breasts sparkled with French decorations. Yet the saints did also remain sufficiently flexible not to fall victim to the popular reaction which overwhelmed the chiefs after 1945.

The end of the second world war brought a series of administrative reforms which promoted other agents of French dominance, elected national politicians and civil servants of the towns. This new elite had mastered the skills (literacy in French, specialised knowledge) upon which modern organisation was based. They were to be intermediaries at new and higher levels between the Senegalese peasant producers, upon whom the economy rests, and the French oil manufacturers who ultimately dominate the economy. The saints not only survived this transition with remarkable dexterity, but used it to increase their power: between the exigencies of the State and the pressures of their own followers, they had learned to walk a political tightrope. And they have yet to show much sign of losing their sense of balance.

NOTES

1 A competent review of this debate can be found in R. Betts, *Assimilation and Association in French Colonial Theory, 1890–1914*, New York: Columbia University Press, 1961.

2 W. Ponty, 'Rapport au Sujet de la Politique Indigène en Afrique Occidentale Française', Jan. 1913, in A.N.S.O.M., AOF I, 19. This outlined a policy later defended by Governors–General Clozel (1915–17) and Brévié (1930–6).

3 See Marty's studies on Mauritania (1916), Senegal (1917), Soudan (1920), Guinea (1921), all published in Paris by Leroux. Also Arnaud, *Précis de Politique Musulmane*, Alger: Jourdain, 1906. Coppolani, *Les Confréries Religieuses Musulmanes* (Alger: Jourdain, 1897) was co-authored with O. Dupont. The French Islamists of this period certainly deserve a full-length study. An introduction can be found in D. Cruise O'Brien, 'Towards an Islamic Policy in French West Africa, 1854–1914', in *Journal of African History*, Vol. VIII, No. 2, 1967.

4 Combes outlines this project in some detail in an official letter of 1902. *Président du Conseil* to *Ministre des Colonies*, 1 Aug. 1902, in A.N.S.O.M., Missions 115F.

5 See for example Father Bouchaud's *L'Eglise en Afrique Noire*, Paris: La Palatine, 1958, pp. 106–7. Also *Bulletin de la Congrégation du Saint-Esprit*, Vol. XXII, 1903–4, pp. 654–6.

6 See P. *Marty, Etudes sur l'Islam au Sénégal*, Paris: Leroux, 1917, Vol. II, pp. 287–8.

7 A. Quellien, *La Politique Musulmane en Afrique Occidentale Française*, Paris: Larose, 1910, p. 100, for an accolade to Islam as a step towards French culture.

8 A sensitive treatment of this problem (in Sierra Leone) is to be found in M. Kilson, *Political Change in a West African State*, Cambridge, Mass.: Harvard University Press, 1966, pp. 9–33.

9 L. V. Thomas, *Les Diola*, Dakar: Institut Français de l'Afrique Noire, 1958, pp. 324–5.

10 R. L. Buell, *The Native Problem in Africa*, London: Cass, 1965 – first published 1928, Vol. I, p. 1020. Also J. Brochier, *La Diffusion du Progrès Technique en Milieu Rural Sénégalais*, Dakar: Ecole Nationale d'Economie Appliquée, 1966, Vol. I, p. 94.

11 'Higher-level' chiefs, with authority over an area equivalent to several

cantons, were recognised in certain instances in the early years of colonial rule. The trend in official policy from the time of Governor General Ponty was to the replacement of these larger units (Provinces) by the standard Canton. On the military principles of French colonial administration see La Documentation Française, *Notes et Etudes Documentaires*, No. 2508, Paris: 1959, p. 8.

12 As outlined in Weber's essay on bureaucracy in H. Gerth and C. Wright Mills (ed. and trans.), *From Max Weber*, London and New York: Oxford University Press, 1946, pp. 196–244.

13 F. G. Bailey, *Stratagems and Spoils*, Oxford: Blackwell, 1969, p. 169.

14 See the B.D.S. newspaper, *Condition Humaine*, 30 August, 1951.

15 See M. Klein, *Islam and Imperialism in Senegal*, Edinburgh: Edinburgh University Press, 1968, p. 153.

16 Buell, *op. cit.* Vol. I, p. 1008.

17 Klein, *op. cit.* p. 194.

18 La Documentation Française, *op. cit.* p. 8.

19 This point is well made, in another context, by J. Suret-Canale, 'La Fin de la Chefferie en Guinée', in *Journal of African History*, Vol. VII, No. 3, 1966.

20 Mamby Sidibé, quoted in G. Snyder, *One-Party Government in Mali*, New Haven: Yale University Press, 1965, p. 12.

21 R. Arnaud, *L'Islam et la Politique Musulmane Française en Afrique Occidentale Française*, Paris: Afrique Française, 1912, p. 9.

22 These *tariqas* each acknowledged a saintly founder, and some elements of a distinct ritual, but organisationally were decentralised into a large number of local lodges. A useful summary can be found in two works by J. S. Trimingham, *Islam in West Africa*, Oxford: Clarendon Press, 1959, pp. 88–101, and *A History of Islam in West Africa*, Oxford: Clarendon Press, 1962, pp. 156–60.

23 C. Geertz, *Islam Observed*, New Haven and London: Yale University Press, 1968, p. 65. Geertz is here concerned with 'scripturalism' in Islam, a literate urban tradition, but the political relevance of his remarks on the subject will extend to Senegal's saints.

24 The death of an important saint usually gave rise to some competition among the sons or even brothers of the deceased, and in this competition to attract the dead man's following there were possibilities for the more intelligent and skilful.

25 'Rapport Sur Amadou Bamba', 30 October 1913, in *Dossier Amadou Bamba*, A.R.S.D.

26 A.R.S.D., 13G.17.17, and *L'Ouest Africain Français*, 13 August 1926.

27 L. Nekkach, 'Le Mouridisme Depuis 1912', St Louis-Sénégal, unpublished, 1952, p. 2.

28 Quoted in Michel Leiris, *L'Afrique Fantôme*, Paris: Gallimard, 1934, p. 147.

29 F. G. Bailey, *Stratagems and Spoils* . . ., p. 77.

4

BUREAUCRATS AND CO-OPERATORS

BUREAUCRATS AND CO-OPERATORS

The organisation of a peanut economy

Recent rural unrest in Senegal, a series of drought years from 1968 to 1973 and a tendency to the rejection of commercial agriculture, have focused much official and even some international journalistic attention on the predicament of the (largely Wolof) peasantry.[1] The fate of Senegal's peasant farmers was of course first decreed by nature, which endowed Senegal with soils so poor as to leave little practical alternative to the peanut as a source of export revenue.[2] Stagnant or declining world market prices for this staple export (accounting consistently for some four fifths of total export value) have not helped. Consequent economic difficulties are in turn gravely exacerbated by a rapid rise in population (officially 2.5% per annum nationally, quite possibly more for the peanut region of the north-west).[3] This causes overcrowding on the land, with over-cultivation and soil exhaustion, and so stimulates migration to towns and cities which can provide few employment outlets.

The Wolof peasantry (who produce two thirds of Senegal's peanut crop) are thus faced with a situation over which their control is necessarily limited, at least for the present and the immediate future. Yet these broad constraints – ecological, demographic, market-economic – for all their ultimate importance, do not in themselves provide anything like a full explanation of the present situation of rural economic crisis and unrest. The Wolof peasants are not only the victims of vast impersonal forces, they are also subordinate elements in a local structure (social, economic, and political) in which they are both disadvantaged and resentful – to varying degrees, depending among other things on the particular agents of dominance involved. Any attempt at an explanation of the present situation (1973) must accordingly take account of the specific social and political evolution of the peasantry, that is, of the *organisational* consequences of the intrusions of the market economy.

In these organisational terms, and from an admittedly rather narrow-minded economic perspective, the Wolof peanut peasants may in local Senegalese terms be seen as victims of a triple exploitation. First there are the Muslim saints, to whom they give a proportion both of their labour time and of the cash produce of their own labour. Second are the private traders who act as intermediaries in handling the peanut crop and providing credit, albeit on the fringes of the law (at best). Third and above all, the state, which now enjoys a legal monopoly of peanut marketing and which draws quite startling profits both legally and through the illicit private initiative of its agents.

These various agencies of dominance are certainly linked one to another, as will be demonstrated below, but cumulatively they make up a systematic pattern which works principally to the advantage of state employees (bureaucrats). Saints in particular, and private traders to a lesser degree, occupy an intermediary position which may serve either to facilitate or to cushion (even obstruct) bureaucratic dominance. The state retains control of the local economy, acting as privileged intermediary for the French oil manufacturers who process the peanut crop (Lesieur and Petersen, most importantly). In local terms, the most stark conflict of economic interest is that between bureaucrat and peasant.

This conflict of interests, to be documented below in

detail, can nonetheless be *too* starkly defined. Dealing in such conceptual terms as '*the* state' and '*the* peasants', one enters a field of (necessary) short-hand or abstraction. Political factionalism serves to promote divisions within both rulers and subjects, while mechanisms of clientage provide ties between particular groups of rulers and subjects. This refinement of the argument is developed in detail in the next essay ('Clans, clienteles and communities'), but at this point one may note that cash does indeed flow downwards as well as upwards (albeit in differential proportions). Were this not the case, the Senegalese political and economic system in all likelihood could not survive.

The political economy of Senegal is here treated, once again, in historical terms. And this of course involves the colonial and post-colonial ties between Senegal and France.[4] French market demands, and French political control, brought the peanut to Senegal as a commercial proposition (a proposition which could scarcely in the circumstances be refused). The concern here however is not with this powerful external agency, rather with the local Senegalese instruments through which French market demands are translated.

Agricultural co-operatives are of the first importance in this latter connection, as the institutions which currently provide the organisational links between the peasantry and the dominant forces both of the economy and the body politic. The present situation of course must be understood against the background of the long history of commercial agriculture in Senegal, and an account of that history here will review the collective agricultural organisations which have in the past been developed by, or imposed upon, the peasantry. Two organisational forms in particular are isolated: firstly, the 'traditional co-operatives' of Wolof society – notably the collective work groups dating back to pre-colonial times and partially surviving today, which are of particular modern relevance in view of the ideological emphasis placed by government leaders on the 'habit of co-operation' as a base on which to build new co-operative institutions; secondly, the mutualist administrative structure developed by the French colonial administration, of modern relevance because it appears to have provided a compelling (although officially repudiated) institutional precedent for Senegalese policy makers after independence in 1960.

The central concern of this essay is nevertheless not with historical precedent, but with the present economic and political effects of the co-operative movement established with Senegal's national independence. Those familiar with the workings of co-operatives elsewhere in Africa will doubtless not be startled to find that the institutionalisation of the government's agricultural development programme has worked conspicuously to the advantage of privileged elements in rural society, often permitting a more authoritarian pattern of local leadership than previously. The argument made here, however, is that local notables were not the major beneficiaries of these institutional innovations. The national bureaucracy and political elite, as already suggested, had much to gain in the establishment of a new framework of political control in the rural areas. The administrative device of the marketing co-operatives, with a resultant state monopoly of the marketing of agricultural produce, were well adapted both to secure political control and to extract a high proportion of total revenues from the peasantry. An official ideology of economic development, of socialist inspiration,[5] provided justification for these levies in terms of the long-run gains to be won by short-run sacrifices. Such an ideology can in certain circumstances perhaps be justified: Barrington Moore, among others, has argued that all programmes of rapid modernisation (capitalist or socialist) appear necessarily to be implemented at the expense of the peasantry – which must be squeezed for its cash surplus to finance the early stages of an industrial revolution.[6] In the Senegalese case, however, the financial 'sacrifices' of peasants appear to be very readily absorbed in the current expenditure of government and of government employees. The cash surplus from commercial agriculture is not, on the whole, allocated to productive investment, and is thus unlikely to result in any long-run 'breakthrough in modernisation'.

The conflict of interest between the cash-cropping peasants and the state apparatus may be identified as a legacy of French colonial rule in Senegal: the present governing class (or elite) is the inheritor, in a thinly disguised version, of the colonial state, and economic and financial relations with France have altered only very slowly since independence. But to point to the broader context, in which peasants may be portrayed as the oppressed elements of an international structure of dependence, should not be to deny a substantial autonomy to the local situation. The Senegalese governing class has its own interests to promote, and these are by no means effectively defined by a subservient relation to France.

Even leaving aside for the moment the important matter of political factionalism, one can note that the precise relation of the state bureaucracy to the governing party remains to be elaborated. For our purposes here, in focusing on the peasantry, the Senegalese ruling class can be treated as a relatively homogenous category, clearly distinguished from the peasantry by income levels, style of life, and access to institutional sources of power in the machinery of state. But it is crucial to this analysis, in dealing with rural co-operative structures, to deal with differentiation and stratification within *rural* society. Many significant bases of differentiation – ethnic, religious, caste – can readily be established, but the principal distinction for this argument is between the mass of peasant producers and that privileged minority which can draw important benefits from participation in the state apparatus (saints, traders, locally 'elected' co-operative officers). This latter distinction is not perhaps a sharply qualitative one, such as that for example between a landlord and a tenant class, but historical processes since French conquest have consistently tended to the stratification of rural society in function of access to administrative resources.

TRADITIONAL CO-OPERATION AND SOCIAL INEQUALITY

Senegalese government spokesmen, in justification of the new official programme of agricultural co-operation initiated in 1960, repeatedly stressed the view that modern co-operative institutions must draw their strength from 'real human communities' with their 'old communitarian values'.[7] The need for a comprehensive modernisation of prior communal forms was clearly recognised, but there remained an ideological emphasis – especially marked in the early 1960s – on the notion of a return to the grass roots of communitarian tradition. Traditional rural solidarity and democracy would help to free the peasants from the exploitation suffered under French colonial rule, granted also the decisive intervention of government to provide a new institutional framework.

The possible adaptation of traditional co-operative forms to the requirements of modern agricultural co-operation has of course been studied in a wide variety of situations, and the cautious to pessimistic view of most recent scholarship on the subject appears to apply only too well to the Senegalese experience. Modern institutionalised co-operation places qualitatively new demands on leaders, through which ties of kinship or friendship readily become the basis of 'corruption' and 'nepotism'. The very category, 'traditional', becomes increasingly illusory with the intrusive effects of a market economy, and with a differentiation between rich and poor farmers which tends to alter the character of collective work. R. P. Dore in a recent study has argued that successful co-operation in a market economy requires at least an 'equalising trend' in peasant society, together with an 'institutionalised suspicion' of co-operative officials on the part of a literate and awakened peasantry.[8] Neither of these conditions were met in Senegal, in the post-colonial period, and in the absence of such an adaptation it would indeed appear that 'traditional' communities provided little effective social basis for the new institutions sponsored by the government.

Evidence from recent studies conducted among the Wolof suggests in any case a cautious view with regard to the present importance of 'traditional communities' in the workings of the agrarian cycle. Large extended kinship groups have tended over time to disintegrate into smaller consumption units, largely under the impact of agricultural commercialisation. Solidary groups for agricultural work do, on the other hand, exist among the Wolof, cutting across class and lineage lines, but they are in general only occasional in activity and restricted in function, while sometimes they are also effectively subservient to saints or traders.

Occasional groups include notably the young men of a given village, who may from time to time come together to perform necessary public works, or perhaps to cultivate a field the harvest of which may be sold to meet the ceremonial expenses of one of the members. Such work allows for a display of strength and manliness before a crowd of admirers, and is often concluded by a feast and party. Groups of neighbours may also form in a village to help out with each other's principal agricultural tasks (especially the harvest), much as farmers do in most parts of the world.

Groups of this kind,[9] the membership of which often shifts from one occasion to another, are very far from stable communities. The absence of large stable working groups among the Wolof seems explicable in terms of the impact of commercial agriculture (now over 150 years old in parts of the Wolof zone). Extended family groups, the economic unity of which is focused more on consumption than on production, have been affected by the same process. The traditional patrilineage, including several compounds, is now of much reduced importance in the commercial sector. Cash-crop farming has promoted the exploitation of land by individual nuclear family units, even by individual family members: a tendency reinforced in some areas by the migration of junior family members (younger brothers) to establish independent farm settlements. The local subsistence crop (millet) is significantly still grown and collectively stored by large extended family units (with dependents), but peanuts may be cultivated and sold individually by the wife, brother, or son of a family head.[10]

'Nuclearisation' and 'individualisation' within large family groups have been accompanied by a growing economic differentiation between more and less successful farmers, at least a potential class differentiation between rural rich and poor. These trends in turn have their impact on 'co-operative' agricultural work: the wealthier members of a local community (traders), who can afford a lavish outlay on entertainment of groups of young men harvesting their fields, thus convert the collective work group into a variant of hired labour. The dependent work group can assume a more or less permanent character in the case of local Muslim peasants who come together to work the fields of their saints (of the Qadiriyya and Tijaniyya as well as Mouride Sufi orders).

COLONIAL PROVIDENCE SOCIETIES: THE ADMINISTRATIVE CLAMP

The *Sociétés de Prévoyance* (Providence Societies), established by the French administration in Senegal through legislation of 1910 (decree of 29 June), and maintained with some modifications until national independence, were designed to provide material services to the African peasantry while maintaining official control over certain aspects of agricultural production.[11] The original legislation gave these societies a partially co-operative character: membership was voluntary, the chief official an (administratively nominated) African. A common fund was established to provide security in the event of natural disaster, while selected seed, fertiliser, and agricultural implements were distributed on relatively easy terms. Through these services the peasant would (it was hoped) be freed of the oppression of usury and debt which had developed with agricultural commercialisation. He would also be able to increase his own and the territory's productivity through the improved farming methods taught by the Society's officers.

These services were indeed valued by some peasants, who even found it advantageous to pay subscriptions and taxes for dependents or fictitious persons in order to benefit from the loans which the Societies provided. The positive incentive to join was nevertheless insufficient to ensure a large membership in most Societies, and in 1915 (decree of 8 January) the government altered the character of the institution by making membership compulsory for all heads of households (a situation which lasted to 1947). Henceforth the President of the Society, *ex officio*, would be the local French administrative officer, the *Commandant de Cercle*. Thus reformed, the Societies were administratively very effective. Van Vollenhoven (Governor General of French West Africa 1917–18) called them 'the best collaborators of governmental action'.[12] Both in the first and second world wars they were particularly useful in requisitioning from the African subjects.

Peasant 'members' of these Societies did not clearly differentiate them from other manifestations of the colonial government: the relatively light annual subscription (about ten to forty pence) was called by them the 'supplementary fine' or 'little tax'. Interest rates on loans provided by the Society (twenty-five per cent), although much lower than those available from private sources (sometimes over one hundred per cent), were high in view of the absence of risk incurred by a lender with such powerful sanctions against defaulters. Many peasants nonetheless must have welcomed even such a partial 'abolition of usury', as the alternative was to sell their crop at a disadvantageous price to private traders and simultaneously to 'purchase' goods on a semi-compulsory basis.

Loans and other assistance provided by the Society were allocated by decision of the French official, and aid seems to have gone preferentially to the most compliant local notables: administratively appointed chiefs, for example, and Muslim saints would be given loans in the names of 'communities' – which were subsequently appropriated on a private basis. Certain Muslim dignitaries, notably the saints of the Mouride brotherhood, were enabled to found huge agricultural estates with the financial and technical assistance of the Providence Societies. Fungicide, fertiliser, food, and seed loans were allocated preferentially to those who were already wealthy and powerful. From the 'productionist' standpoint of the colonial administration it was of course more profitable to assist those who already had the means (in land and labour) to make use of such assistance, than to bail out impoverished farmers who could barely meet the needs of themselves and their dependents. The result of this policy was that the 'subscriptions' of the

Society's poorer members served partially to finance those who had established local dominance, thus reinforcing existing social inequalities.

The Providence Society remained the dominant institution of agricultural administration throughout the colonial period. Ten Societies were established to cover the entire area of Senegal in the years 1910–12, and total membership eventually (1958) rose to over a million (1,166,000).[13] The functions of the institution grew steadily more extensive over time: an important change was made in 1933 (decree of 9 November) when the Societies were empowered to buy and sell agricultural produce (the great bulk of the trade none the less remained in private hands throughout the colonial period).[14] Farm implements and fertiliser were distributed in quantity: 40,000 seeders, 3,000 mechanical hoes, 1,500 ploughs, and more than 30,000 tons of chemical fertiliser in the years 1948–58.[15] Tens of thousands of tons of peanut seeds were distributed each year, an increasing proportion from selected varieties: seed distribution just before sowing time helped to overcome the 'improvidence' of the poorer peasants, who had previously often eaten or sold that proportion of their crop which should have been stored for seed.

The administrative character (and the name) of the Society was formally altered in the transitional period leading up to Senegalese independence, under pressure from the newly elected national politicians. In 1947 and 1953 the principle of voluntary membership was restored, and provision made for a management committee with an elected majority. Further reform followed, which did little, apparently, to mitigate the effective dominance of local French officials. In 1960 the Societies were formally abolished, to be replaced by the new structures of Senegalese independence. There none the less remained a real continuity, in terms both of personnel and of basic administrative method: the precedent of the Providence Societies was to do much to shape the workings of the complex of new institutions elaborated by the Senegalese government's legislation of 1960.[16]

INDEPENDENCE AND THE NATIONAL DEVELOPMENT PROGRAMME

Entanglement at the grass roots

Colonial administrative practice thus had tended to complement market forces in promoting new forms of stratification within rural society. In view of this differentiation there can be little occasion for surprise in the superficially paradoxical results of the Senegalese government's decision in 1960 to seek a new rural development at the 'grass roots'. In most villages in the Wolof zone it was already the case that a minority of households controlled the major part of the cultivable land: 10 out of 33 in one example studied, 12 out of 102 in another group of five villages.[17] Successful adaptation to commercial farming had enabled some to expand their holdings, while others could scarcely afford to pay annual tribute to a local notable for a right to cultivate. Wealthier landholders had reinforced their dominance by lending to the less well endowed, and sometimes also by handling trade between the village and the outside world.

Inequalities of a political nature were no less significant. Great advantages (as we have seen) had accrued to those chiefs and saints who had acted as intermediaries between the French and the Wolof peasantry. These relatively privileged legatees of colonial rule had in many cases secured control of crucial economic and political resources in the transitional period prior to Senegalese independence. [The relation of such a 'new class' to pre-colonial Wolof stratification patterns is admittedly ambiguous, although one may safely advance the generalisation that colonial rule had promoted a fairly drastic re-ordering of Wolof society.]

Existing forms of social differentiation were naturally enough reflected in the forms assumed by the new co-operative movement in Senegal. National political leaders were indeed aware of some of the contradictions involved in such a context in imposing a nominally democratic, egalitarian institution. Official references to the Senegalese 'tradition of co-operation' did not disregard the alarming precedent of the period 1947–53, when there had been a brief efflorescence of privately constituted marketing co-operatives.[18] These in effect became alliances of rural notables (chiefs, saints, traders, party representatives) for the pursuit of private gain. Clients of these dignitaries were expected to join and sell their harvest to the 'co-operative' so that dependence on the patron was increased. Local notables regarded the institution as their private property: in one case 3,000 subscriptions were paid by 10 dignitaries – in the names of both the living and the dead. Such co-operatives were informally affiliated to one or other of the major political parties of the period, and were used to channel 'loans' from these sources – 'loans which were used above all to satisfy the personal needs of the director – purchase of buildings, of automobiles or trucks, loans to third parties, financing of commercial projects'.[19] The experience of these 'co-operatives' of political and commercial activists indicated some of the likely problems in extending co-operatives on a nation-wide basis.

The Senegalese government's response to these perceived problems at independence was contained in the community development programme of 'Rural Animation', originally conceived with a view to bringing about a new peasant consciousness which would undermine the dominance of a nascent rural bourgeoisie. This initiative in the direction of a rural 'African Socialism' appeared to have been effectively checked with the downfall of its political sponsor, Mamadou Dia, in 1962: his downfall was a victory for the already dominant elements of Senegalese society over a small but active group of radical civil servants and intellectuals.[20] The Animation movement subsequently became almost moribund, and the new official movement of marketing co-operatives (launched in 1960) again tended to benefit above all the already privileged.

The new co-operatives were established throughout rural Senegal by government initiative in the early 1960s.[21] Their functions were to be effectively restricted to three related areas: provision of credit, supply of agricultural implements and other materials, marketing of members' produce. Supplies and sales all involved members on an individual basis, and the existing conditions of agricultural production were not directly affected. The proclaimed purpose of this programme of co-operation was to end the exploitationary evils of the colonial marketing system, which had maintained peasants in semi-permanent indebtedness.[22] These were of course the same durable evils which the colonial Providence Societies had been established to combat half a century previously. The formally democratic procedures of the new institutions, in which officers were to be elected and controlled by a general assembly of members, scarcely prevented local influentials from seizing control. Wealthy members could do this by paying subscriptions for their clients, for example, but in general they relied on prestige and power in the community to win uncontested control. The less well endowed members often resigned themselves to the idea that the co-operative was 'not their affair', while management councils rarely or never met.

Co-operative officials, nominally elected but effectively often chosen as local notables by government, were thus in a position to turn the institution to their own economic purposes. These officials, drawn where possible from the literate minority, were able to profit from their status as privileged intermediaries. A wide variety of illicit arrangements came rapidly to flourish, notably involving the two crucial offices of President and Weigher. One author, after a meticulous examination of fraudulent practices, claimed to have established a provisional total of 142 distinct variants of graft in the state marketing institutions.[23] Some of these arrangements, such as the elementary device of the false weighing scales, had a long history in the Senegalese peanut trade. Others developed in the co-operative's transactions with the government, especially in connection with the various government services which were channeled to the peasants through co-operative officials. Agricultural credit, relief food supplies, medical supplies, refunds on the sale of crops, all became objects either of commercial speculation or of differential distribution to those with kinship or other ties to officials.[24] The enforcement of a form of collective responsibility for bad debts to the government meant, furthermore, that the mass of members made good deficits which arose in part from illicit speculation on the part of the local notables. Economic inequalities in rural society were thus strongly reinforced by the co-operatives, as in the past by the Providence Societies. There is of course nothing particularly unusual here in terms of the experience of co-operative movements elsewhere. H. A. Landsberger in another context has identified this model as that of the co-operative path to capitalism.[25]

Bureaucratic hegemony

Senegal under French rule had of course been a relatively favoured colony, in which official doctrines of 'assimilation' to French culture were applied at least to the extent of providing educational institutions for the training of an urban African elite. This elite, a large one at least in comparison with other French colonies, found employment outlets within the administrative structure of the French

West African Federation. The capital and central bureaucracy of the Federation were located in Senegal, at Dakar, and Senegalese clerks were exported to other colonies in the Federation where educational services were less advanced. The disintegration of the French West African Federation in 1958, and the separate independence of the individual colonies in 1960, thus left the Senegalese state only too well endowed with trained bureaucratic manpower. Separate independence meant that each new state gave employment preference to its own nationals, with the consequence that the overseas Senegalese were rapidly repatriated to swell the ranks of the bureaucratic semi-employed remaining in the former Federal capital. The financial burden which these officials placed on the new Senegalese state was all the greater in view of the large wage increases which had been granted in the terminal phase of colonial rule (notably by the second 'Lamine Guèye' law of 1950). Thus at independence salaries in the public sector were over seven times higher than the estimated average peasant household revenue, while ten years after independence (in 1970) official statistics showed that over half (52.5%) of annual government expenditure was devoted to civil service salaries.[26] These salaries have indeed been frozen since independence, but with stagnant peanut prices the same effectively applies to peasant revenue (22 francs CFA (Communauté Financière Africaine) per kilo 1963–7, 18 francs 1968–70, 23 francs 1971–3).[27] Revenue in recent years has indeed been subject to substantial net decline, marketed totals dropping from an annual average of 830,000 tons (1961–8) to 550,000 tons with bad climatic conditions from 1969 to 1973.[28] And over the same period one statistic at least shows a sturdy growth, that for government employees. Some 10,000 apparently in 1959–60, 20,100 civil servants and 14,800 government 'auxiliaries' in 1965, 40,000 civil servants and 21,000 semi-public auxiliaries in 1973. In

1973 the total number[29] of civil service and civil service-related employees (61,000) very nearly equalled the total for all other forms of wage employment in Senegal (63,000). And although real peasant household revenues, taking account of subsistence crops and illicit sales below market prices, are impossible to calculate with any degree of precision, it can be safely asserted that civil servants in 1973 were not less than seven times, and very probably over ten times better off than peasant farmers. Even skilled workers come substantially behind the low-level 'auxiliaries' in government service – figures in 1965: civil servants £1,500 p.a., auxiliaries £660, skilled workers £504, peasants at most £200 – including subsistence produce.[30] [Lest a moralising posture on this author's part be implied with regard to such figures, be it noted that a London university lecturer earns more (legally at least) than a Senegalese cabinet minister.] Granted this reservation, the implications of these figures are dramatic enough. And even official statistics for 'legal' incomes, or 'normal' revenues, consistently distort the picture: the law in Senegal is very fragile, and where it is infringed, illegality works in immediate income terms to the advantage of bureaucrats and to the disadvantage of most peanut producers.

Partial nationalisation of the peanut trade at independence (1960), with the elaboration of an administrative hierarchy to control the economy, served among other things to absorb the surplus Senegalese personnel of the French West African Federation in the name of 'national development' and 'African Socialism': it also helped to eliminate the French and Lebanese businessmen who had dominated the peanut trade in the interior in favour of Senegalese nationals. A state marketing board (*Office de Commercialisation Agricole* – O.C.A.) was established, essentially to purchase the peanut crop from the producers and sell to the French processors in Dakar. The O.C.A. at the capital and regional centres worked through a subordinate agency (now entitled *Office National de Co-opération et d'Assistance pour le Développement* – O.N.C.A.D.) at the smaller towns. Below the O.N.C.A.D., at the point of contact between the bureaucracy and the peasantry, were the newly established agricultural co-operatives.[31] While the co-operative movement increased the institutional resources of rural notables, therefore, it should be emphasised that these resources were made available by the national government. The rural privileged element indeed appears as very much the subordinate partner in the governing alliance with urban politicians and bureaucrats. Co-operatives had involved local notables in a national apparatus of economic and political control, an institutional grid in the rural areas which could take over from the out-going colonial administration. The licit and illicit benefits which accrued to the rural notables may indeed be seen as the price of their acquiescence in the higher graft of their official superiors.

The political objectives of the Co-operative Programme were partially recognised by its Director in 1962 in discussing the purposes of the legislation of 1960: 'the major pre-occupation of the Government of Senegal was initially to organise the rural world.' This pre-occupation, he declared, explained 'the originality of the Senegalese formula' of co-operation . . . 'while as a general rule co-operatives across the world are born of the producers' desires, in Senegal since independence they have been the work of the government . . .'[32] A dubious originality perhaps, but comparison is scarcely relevant here.

Official initiative from 1960 onwards brought a very rapid diffusion of the co-operative movement: 679 co-operatives had been established within a year (1961), 1,563 within five years (1965).[33] The rapid success of the movement is explained in the following description of an apparently typical example.

'In 1960, the (government) co-operative officer of the locality called together the chiefs of the villages of X, Y and Z, and informed them of the desire, or rather the will, of the administration that a co-operative should be created among the inhabitants of the three villages. This was the law.'[34]

The location of these multi-village co-operative centres, equally, was decided not in accordance with local demands, but rather in view of communications access which would facilitate transport of the harvest to regional centres.

Individual membership of the co-operatives remained voluntary in principle. By a series of measures, however, notably including the gradual suppression of licenses to private peanut traders, the government by 1968 had made it necessary for virtually all commercial farmers to join a co-operative in order to sell their crops. Membership by 1966 included 80 per cent of compound heads in the peanut-producing region.[35] These family heads then often sold on behalf of their individual dependents, although recently it has increasingly become the practice for individual family members to join the co-operative. 'Membership' in the co-operative, as in the colonial Providence Societies, did not of course imply any effective control of the institution from below. Democratic assemblies of members (certainly those which I witnessed) were usually rather silent gatherings, held only in the presence of government officials who could ensure that popular decisions were in conformity with administrative regulations.

Administrative control of the co-operatives not only served a political function, in 'organising the rural world'. Co-operative marketing institutions also enabled the state bureaucracy to appropriate a large part of the revenue derived from commercial agriculture, to make legal and illegal profits on a scale at least rivalling that of the private traders of the colonial period. A single national peanut price was fixed each year by the national marketing board

(O.C.A.), initially with a differential for distance from export ports. This price has consistently been fixed at a level which allows a substantial margin of profit to the O.C.A. in reselling to French buyers. Even in strictly legal terms, the net profit to the state may exceed the price paid to the producer. Thus one senior official (unofficially) provided these figures for peanut marketing in 1971: price to peasants at co-operative, 19.5 francs CFA per kilo; price charged by O.C.A. to oil manufacturers, *c.* 40 francs; marketing costs to state (inclusive), 4 francs; export tax on oil (equivalence to kilo in shell), 5.5 francs. This would leave a net profit to the state (not allowing for the cost of levying the export duty) of 22 francs CFA per kilo. Such figures are indeed contested by other sources, although correspondence with Senegalese government officials and French oil manufacturers failed to elicit any official verdict (or even a reply). One semi-official source did however (in 1973) suggest that the O.C.A. price was 'too high', and when pressed volunteered an estimated price of 38 francs. And an economist working in Senegal, without attributing his source, gives a much lower figure (32 francs).[36] State 'marketing costs' also give rise to divergent estimates, from 5 to 9 francs per kilo: various sources nonetheless at least concur in a verdict that 'costs' over 5 francs enter the realm of inefficiency or corruption (possibly a combination of the two).

These official figures, albeit the subject of some possible controversy, in any case have only an approximate correspondence with the real workings of the state marketing system. Payments to the co-operators, at least since 1968, have been made not in cash but in credit chits which may be redeemed after the peanuts have been resold to the French companies. The delay involved, of three or four months, is a serious imposition on the very tight economic situation of most peasants, and it is not surprising that the credit chits have become the objects of usurious speculation on the part of private traders who can advance hard cash. This practice has indeed become very widely prevalent, and the traders' price apparently can be in the region of 12 francs per kilo, allowing a profit margin close to a hundred per cent in four months. Such traders are at least nominal members of a co-operative, from which they can redeem credit chits. Most significantly for this analysis, they often act for senior government officials who provide funds and political protection in such illicit activities while also, of course, taking a substantial cut from the hundred per cent profit.

Even the low official price in turn leaves an optimistic impression even of the amount legally received by the farmer. There are then the deductions made for the agricultural implements, seed, fungicide, and fertiliser ordered by the co-operative member: prices for implements and services in general allow the government a profit margin. These deductions are of course in principle a means of providing a service to the peasants (instalment buying), but they become onerous where co-operative members are forced to buy agricultural equipment which they did not themselves order, as can happen, for example, where an administrative officer wishes to conform to goals set out in the plan.[37] Peasants who cannot afford the instalments frequently re-sell or pawn their equipment to private traders at a much reduced value. Either way this avenue can offer no more than a short-run cash escape. The scale of official and other levies is such that peasants are in a state of semi-permanent indebtedness, to the co-operative and often also to private traders, in clear continuity with colonial tradition.

The official peanut price to co-operators, in view of the various charges for services, may itself be substantially below the apparent norm. A report of 1970 estimated that peasants may then effectively (in official terms) have received a price of 10 to 11 francs CFA per kilo out of a nominal 17.50 CFA.[38] A surplus rebate (*ristourne*), in principle of ten per cent on the peanut price, does little in effect to redress this situation. The *ristourne* was paid in full only in the early years of the co-operative programme, when the government wished to attract new members. More recently it has been subject to a whole range of official deductions, which in effect mean that the maximum received by any co-operator is below one quarter of the official ten per cent. These deductions include a levy for development funds, supposedly lodged in the co-operative's account at a government bank, but now by public admission consumed in the current expenditure of national administration.

Surplus revenue, of course, goes to support the government apparatus, or rather to support its employees. A proportion is simply misappropriated by government officials at various levels: the corruption of Senegalese civil servants, frequently condemned by President Senghor, reaches alarming proportions. The very use of the term 'corruption' (as argued in the 'Conclusion' below) is questionable in circumstances where such transactions are the unacknowledged norm for those involved. Thus one observer has estimated that 'losses' and acknowledged fraud in the central marketing board (O.C.A.) in 1965 accounted for more than annual net profit.[39] Lax accounting techniques, dishonest agents, inadequate supervision, all make possible a network of private appropriation in the nationalised marketing sector. The high cost of administration to the citizen is compounded by inefficiency, which has compelled the political leaders to seek administrative assistance from France and elsewhere to promote its rural programme. The national political leadership has frequently condemned this high cost, but salary freezes and reductions in official perks are effectively negated by bureaucratic graft.

The extent of central control over marketing co-operatives has been justified (by some government officials) as necessary to help the illiterate peasants to help themselves. Yet in view of some of the practices reviewed above, and in view of the widely decried and continuing failure to provide members with the necessary education in co-operative management, these 'developmental grounds' become increasingly illusory. With the decline of the Rural Animation programme following the fall of Mamadou Dia in 1962, the marketing co-operatives appear to revert to colonial precedent: Dia himself, just before his fall, had warned of the danger that co-operatives might become a mere 'excrescence of technical administrative services'.[40] Even this 'danger' now seems something of a technocratic utopia, and as peasant incomes decline or at best stagnate, it is increasingly clear that government bureaucracy (or in other terms the ruling elite) is more parasitic on peasant production than 'generative of agrarian progress'.

CONCLUSION. PEASANT REACTION

The mass of peanut-producing peasants (two thirds of them Wolof), who produce some eighty per cent of the country's export revenue, may readily be identified as the victims of the national development programme. Are they then to be seen as an exploited class? There can be little doubt, given some of the figures already cited, of their being exploited, but of course a class designation, such as is employed at various points in the above argument, implies not only a common 'objective' condition but also some common consciousness of that condition. What subjective elements of class consciousness have developed as the peasants react to their predicament? No simple answer is possible to such questions, but certain tendencies do at least emerge. Thus the prevalent spirit, until quite recently, has been one of resignation: the word 'development' has been popularly identified with administrative will, and one local chief spoke for most when he declared of the co-operators that 'We are the Government's captives'.[41] The reactions of co-operators of course have also varied with the extent to which individuals manage to derive particular (usually illicit) benefits from their participation in the government system. The evident, even flagrant malpractices of local administrative officials were widely resented, but peasants interviewed by this author in 1967 often reflected wryly that they might themselves act similarly if placed in such a position.

Subsequently, and especially in the years 1969–70, rural dissatisfaction became more sharply defined. Some peasants evaded the government's economic control by smuggling their harvest across the border to Gambia, where peanuts were bought at a higher price (23 francs CFA per kilo in 1971, 3.5 francs over the Senegalese rate) and in cash. This 'peanut-running' has a long history, but it reached a very large scale in this period: 50,000 tons in 1970, almost one tenth of the harvest and a financial loss to the Senegalese state of one and a half million pounds.[42] Other peasants responded to low prices simply by abandoning (or relatively disfavouring) the cultivation of peanuts: this appears to be a large part of the explanation for the bad harvest of 1970 (525,000 tons marketed), despite good climatic conditions and adequate distribution of seed. Bad weather and low prices in other recent years (1968, 1969, 1971) combined to bring about a disastrous fall in peanut production. Farmers have in many cases reverted to millet cultivation, in a broad move from commercial to subsistence agriculture.

Such a 'revolt against the peanut' has been a source of serious disquiet to the national government, which of course is financially almost entirely dependent on peanut revenue. Disaffection was indeed directed not merely at the harmless peanut, but at the co-operative system which the peasants apparently held responsible for their troubles, and at the regime itself. It was ominous for the government that peasant resentment seemed to be directed more at the national elite, which instigated the co-operative programme, than against the local notables who have turned the programme to their particular ends.[43] These notables may profit at the expense of their clients, but they are at least culturally and organisationally integrated within rural society – unlike the 'alien' bureaucrat from the town. In other terms, the bureaucrats of the O.C.A. and O.N.C.A.D. are oriented primarily to private financial gain, and do not indulge in the patronage expenditures which can make local notables acceptable to their clientele (truer admittedly of saints than of traders).

The co-operative movement, in view of this dangerously spreading peasant reaction, appeared by 1970 to be in a state of acute crisis. Government leaders then publicly recognised a need for institutional changes. Thus the Prime Minister, Abdou Diouf, maintained in interview (August 1970) that

> We must reform the co-operatives before the next harvest, or else allow the peasants to sell their peanuts where they please. If we cannot restore the system, then we must put it in question.

President Senghor in a declaration of the same period spoke of the need to 'struggle against the bureaucratic machine' and held that 'it is both right and efficient to allow pressure from the peasantry against the party and government machinery'.[44] In truth government leaders, however genuine their indignation, had little choice in the matter. Peanut harvests had fallen drastically, from the fairly steady marketed average of over 800,000 tons for the years 1961–8, to an average close to 550 tons in the three succeeding years (bad weather a largely contributing factor). Peanut producers, thus impoverished, could afford to ask less than one third of the annual official credit which they had requested three years before (three million pounds in 1967, less than eight hundred thousand pounds in 1970). Of outstanding peasant debts to the co-operatives, some twenty per cent were unpaid in 1970. To this crisis the government had several responses, of varying consequence. In the first place it simply 'cancelled' outstanding co-operative debts, with the help of a three million pound subsidy from the European Development Fund (an encouragement of course to bad debtors, disproportionately the rural notables). In the second place it sought the 'technical assistance' of an Italian consulting organisation, Italconsult, which reported through a series of weighty documents that the co-operatives should be 're-grouped' into larger centres and that marketing personnel (in the co-operatives themselves and in the O.N.C.A.D.) should be thoroughly trained in sound organisational principles. A notion worth examination: Italian lecturers to teach the Senegalese to be incorruptible.[45] In the third place, however, the government did have something serious to offer, an official price increase, from 19.5 francs CFA per kilo (1970 harvest) to 23.1 francs (the standard price for the harvests of 1971–3). This increase was agreed at least partially under pressure from some of the most notable Muslim saints – speaking for themselves as 'large-scale producers' and for their peasant disciples.

The political usefulness of the co-operative movement to the government might thus appear to have been eroded since independence. In the early 1960s the co-operatives did indeed allow the government to achieve the same ends in controlling rural life as had been achieved by the discredited colonial Providence Societies – 'Socialism' then even provided rhetorical justification for the introduction of institutions which went much further than the Providence Societies in drawing off the economic surplus of peasant production. The co-operatives also (at least after 1962) enabled the national bureaucratic and party leaders to consolidate an alliance with rural notables, those who had already gained under colonial rule and who now were to secure increased local political control and economic benefits in managing the new institutions.

The mass of peasant producers indeed have few economic or political resources, with established rural leaders already partially committed to the state apparatus. They do nonetheless have the means of an effective passive resistance to the state. When economic impositions become altogether excessive, as in recent years, they can withdraw from the commercial sector and revert to subsistence farming (millet rather than peanuts). Such a choice certainly offers no long-run solution to the dire material problems of the Senegalese peasantry, but in all the circumstances described above it is rational enough.

NOTES

1 An attention heightened of late by the acute drought and semi-famine to famine conditions of 1972–3, which have brought newspaper reports on Senegal to readers who may scarcely have heard of the country before (unenviable notoriety). Somewhat earlier, in August 1970, a series of articles by Philippe Decraene in *Le Monde* gave a detailed and very well informed review of the then spreading crisis of Senegalese agriculture.

For statistics on peanut production since independence, the principal official sources are the *Bulletin Economique et Statistique de la République du Sénégal* and the annual *Situation Economique et Statistique du Sénégal* (both published in Dakar).

2 But see S. Amin, *L'Afrique de l'Ouest Bloquée*, Paris: Eds. de Minuit, 1971, pp. 23–64, for a more optimistic view. A realistic economic policy should (in Amin's opinion) emphasise coastal fisheries, pastoralism instead of peanut farming throughout most of the country, with commercial agriculture restricted to three areas: Senegal River valley (rice), Niayes region near the Cape Verde peninsula (market gardening), Casamance region (various tropical produce). Co-operation with the neighbouring state of Mauritania, which unlike Senegal has large reserves of minerals (copper notably) could be a basis for future industrial expansion.

There are indeed long-term possibilities for a policy along these lines, but at least a few reservations should be stated. Fisheries on an export scale would require a very substantial capital outlay, were Senegal to compete with the European trawlers already off her coast. Pastoralism throughout the present peanut zone would imply a massive movement of population out of the peanut area, which would need to be quite elaborately planned and (quite probably) implemented by force. There is no Stalin on the Senegalese horizon. Rice growing in the Senegal river valley has already been tried, on an experimental basis, and has proved on the whole a costly failure. Industrial co-operation with Mauritania, using the latter's minerals, is more clearly to Senegalese than Mauritanian advantage: Mauritanian leaders are likely to be extremely cautious about any such project.

I only hope, nonetheless, that the future may prove me wrong and Amin right.

3 For the Wolof zone there is suggestive evidence of a rate of increase closer to 3% (3.2% in the village of Missirah, studied by Jean Copans). J. Copans, 'Stratification Sociale et Organisation du Travail Agricole dans les Villages Wolof Mourides du Sénégal', Paris, Ecole Pratique des Hautes Etudes, Thèse de 3e cycle, 1973 (unpublished) p. 109. The starvation of the past two years (1972–3) bringing high infant and child mortality is in the circumstances a more or less inevitable product of population growth. These conditions at present appear to be at their worst (for the Wolof) in the zone around Louga (Region of Diourbel).

4 For an excellent study of this relationship, see Rita Cruise O'Brien, *White Society in Black Africa. The French of Senegal*, London: Faber, 1972.
5 This ideology was elaborated at the time of independence, notably by the then Prime Minister, Mamadou Dia, and by the team of economists responsible for the drafting of the first national development plan. The dominant influence in this team was that of the French Catholic Socialist, Father Lebret. For a statement of their views, see Sénégal, République du, *Rapport Général sur les Perspectives de Développement du Sénégal*, Dakar, CINAM, 1960.
6 Barrington Moore, Jr., *Social Origins of Dictatorship and Democracy. Lord and Peasant in the Making of the Modern World*, Boston: Beacon Press, 1967, pp. 385–6 and throughout.
7 Mamadou Dia writing in 1962, cited in M. Camboulives, *L'Organisation Co-opérative au Sénégal*, Paris: Eds. Pedone, 1967, p. 338.
8 R. P. Dore, 'Traditional Communities and Modern Co-operatives', in P. Worsley (ed.), *Two Blades of Grass*, Manchester: Manchester University Press, 1971. Dore's notion of an 'equalising trend' in particular implies movement away from ascribed, authoritarian leadership patterns.
9 For details of such groups, see D. Ames, 'Wolof Co-operative Work Groups' in W. R. Bascom and M. J. Herskovits (eds.), *Continuity and Change in African Cultures*, Chicago: University of Chicago Press, 1959. Also P. Couty and J. Copans, *Travaux Collectifs Agricoles en Milieu Wolof Mouride*, Dakar: O.R.S.T.O.M., 1968. A more stable form of co-operative work group, the *dimböli* is discussed in G. Rocheteau, *Système Mouride et Rapports Sociaux Traditionnels*, Dakar: O.R.S.T.O.M., 1969.
10 On family and compound structures see Ames; also M. Mergane, 'Rapport sur les Co-opératives dans l'Arrondissement de Ndame', Dakar: Ecole Nationale d'Economie Appliquée, 1965 (unpublished thesis); and of course the remarks in 'Land, Cash and Charisma', above.
11 K. E. Robinson, '*The Sociétés de Prévoyance* in French West Africa' in *Journal of African Administration*, Vol. II, 1950.
12 Cited in A. Ly, *L'Etat et la Production Paysanne*, Paris: Présence Africaine, 1958, p. 38.
13 Ly, pp. 52–5. This membership figure accounts for well over one third of Senegal's population at the time, and for half the estimated total in the agricultural sector.
14 For example, only 14,000 tons of a total peanut harvest of 551,000 tons was sold through the Providence Societies in 1954. Sénégal, Territoire du, *Rapport sur L'Activité des Services*, Dakar, 1954, p. 13.
15 Ly, pp. 46–52.
16 The title of the Providence Society was changed with the 1953 reform, becoming *Société Mutuelle de Production Rurale*, and again in 1956, becoming *Société Mutuelle de Développement Rurale* (S.M.D.R.). After 1956 a restricted movement of officially sponsored co-operatives was launched under the auspices of the S.M.D.R., and this in many ways was to serve as an experimental base for the Senegalese government's 1960 reforms. See Camboulives, pp. 13–59.
17 Information on a case study in the Saloum region provided by M. Vaillant in Kaolack. There are no national landholding statistics, but one can see a broad spread from the estates of hundreds (even thousands) of acres controlled by community notables, to the plots of ten to twenty acres controlled by peasant households. Wolof land holding practices are reviewed in T. Bedu, *Cours de Droit: Legislation Foncière*, Bambey Sénégal: Ecole Nationale des Cadres Ruraux, 1964.

18 See Camboulives, pp. 22–6. In the season 1951–2, at the time of their maximum diffusion, there were 214 such co-operatives, marketing 45,000 tons of peanuts.

19 L. Nekkach, 'Le Mouridisme depuis 1912', St Louis–Sénégal, 1952 (unpublished, preserved in A.R.S.D.). The competing political parties of the time were L. S. Senghor's *Bloc Démocratique Sénégalais* and Lamine Guèye's Socialist Party (S.F.I.O.).

20 P. Thibaud, 'Dia, Senghor, et le Socialisme Africain', in *Esprit*, No. 9, Sept. 1963.

21 For the legislation establishing the co-operatives and other state marketing institutions, see *Journal Officiel de la République du Sénégal*, special number of 30 May 1960.

22 For details on the colonial marketing system, see X. Guiraud, *L'Arachide Sénégalaise*, Paris: Librairie Technique et Economique, 1937, esp. pp. 52–3.

23 J. M. Yung, 'Aperçus sur le Système Co-operatif Sénégalais', Dakar: S.A.T.E.C., 1966 (unpublished report).

24 J. C. Reverdy, *Une Société Rurale au Sénégal: les Structures Foncières, Familiales, et Villageoises des Serer*, Aix-en-Provence: Centre Africain des Sciences Humaines Appliquées, 1968, pp. 100–1. The Serer tribe produce some one quarter of the Senegalese harvest, and together with the Wolof account for over 90% of the national total.

25 H. A. Landsberger, 'Social and Political Preconditions for Co-operatives among poor farmers in the United States South', in P. Worsley (ed.), *Two Blades of Grass . . .*

26 Sénégal, République du, *Situation Economique du Sénégal*, Dakar, 1970, p. 178. Also I.R.F.E.D., 'Le Sénégal en marche', *Les Cahiers Africains*, No. 5, 1962, p. 18.

27 Annual prices in detail: 1963–7, 22.75 francs CFA per kilo sold in Dakar, 22.00 per kilo in Kaolack, 21.75 francs in Ziguinchor (differential to allow for transport costs); 1968, for the same three towns, 18.44 CFA, 17.97, 16.59; 1969, 17.50, 17.10, 15.30 (transport differentials to southern Senegal markedly rising). 1970, a national producer price of 17.00 francs per kilo. In 1971 the national price rose to 19.50 francs, and in 1972 and 1973 was maintained at 23.10 francs CFA per kilo.

28 Annual marketed totals again in detail: 1961, 786,000 tons of peanuts in shell; 1962, 868,000 tons; 1963, 761,000 tons; 1964, 803,000 tons; 1965, 843,000 tons; 1966, 980,000 tons (the peak year); 1967, 741,000 tons; 1968, 818,000 tons; 1969, 604,000 tons; 1970, 525,000 tons, 1971, 450,000 tons (lower than 1930, when 508,000 tons were sold); 1972, 769,000 tons; 1973, 428,000 tons (lowest total since independence). In each case the *marketed* total is for the year following the harvest (marketing going from November of each year to March of the next). These figures make dismal reading when one recalls the objective for 1973 of the third national development plan – a harvest of 1,420,000 tons of peanuts.

29 I.R.F.E.D., for 1959–60 figures. Sénégal, Conseil Economique et Social, 'Note sur la Situation Agricole du Sénégal', Dakar, 1966, Annexe No. 31 (unpublished) for 1965 figures. 1973 figures provided very kindly, after compilation of official documentation on the subject, by M. R. Bourdil of the Sécrétariat d'Etat aux Affaires Etrangères Chargé de la Co-opération, Paris.

30 Sénégal, Conseil Economique et Social (in principle a confidential report, in fact quite readily available). This report deplores the absence of reliable data on peasant incomes since independence, and cites a number of unpublished monographs as suggestive evidence that real peasant incomes

may often be no more than one half the official figure.

31 For details on the administrative procedures involved in the establishment of these institutions, see Camboulives, especially pp. 279–302.

32 A. Ndiaye, 'L'Assistance aux Co-opératives, leur Développement', in *Développement et Civilisations* (special number), 1962, p. 50.

33 These figures include the pre-co-operative institutions called *Associations d'Intérêt Rural,* which did not differ from the co-operatives proper in any significant way.

34 Reverdy, p. 91.

35 Yung, p. 18.

36 Amin, p. 36.

37 Mergane, p. 16.

38 Report of the Senegalese *Conseil Economique et Social*, 1970, cited in *Le Monde*, 20 August 1970.

39 Yung, p. 33.

40 Cited in Ndiaye, p. 52.

41 Quoted in Reverdy, p. 94.

42 See *Le Monde*, 22 August 1970.

43 See Philippe Decraene's articles entitled 'Le Sénégal, dix ans après l'Indépendance', *Le Monde*, 20–3 August 1970.

44 Both quotations given by Decraene, *Le Monde*, 21 August 1970.

45 I cannot recommend the reader to see ITALCONSULT, *Réorganisation de l'O.N.C.A.D., Rapport Général sur la Co-opération,* Rome, 1969, 1970, as the report (the basis of statistical information in this paragraph) remains quite strictly unavailable. The reader may indeed spare himself the considerable trouble involved in securing access to this document: in great bulk it is no more than an unusually verbose reiteration of well-known problems, offering only rather pedantic bureaucratic 'solutions'.

5

CLANS, CLIENTELES AND COMMUNITIES

CLANS, CLIENTELES AND COMMUNITIES

A structure of political loyalties

INTRODUCTION

'The clan is a Senegalese evil, which has been with us for long generations, constantly denounced by the party, but always increasing in strength'. This official verdict reflects an unofficial consensus, that 'clans' are the effective units of political competition in the Senegalese single-party state: 'in almost every region, we witness passionate confrontation, occasionally armed struggle, between clans which all claim affiliation to the governing party'.[1] It should be made clear that the 'clan' in local Franco-Senegalese parlance has nothing or very little in common with the normal usage of the term among social anthropologists. The modern political clan is not defined by kinship, real or imagined, although kinship relations may exist and may help to reinforce political solidarity within a given clan group: there is no requirement for a common revered ancestor, real or imagined; no clanic name; no shared taboo; no role of exogamy. The clan is a political faction, operating within the institutions of the state and the governing party: it exists above all to promote the interests of its members through political competition, and its first unifying principle is the prospect of the material rewards of political success. Political office and the spoils of office are the very definition of success: loot is the clanic totem.

The prevalent practice of 'clan' politics in Senegal makes for a situation of a type quite familiar to political scientists, that of the 'spoils system'. The patron-client relationship, which is at the core of the clan, is also one which has been very widely discussed in other countries: some scholars even claim a more or less universal applicability for the model of political clientelism.[2] The factional politics decried by the Senegalese Minister of the Interior certainly do not constitute a specifically Senegalese problem ('*un mal Sénégalais*'). But situations of a broadly similar type do retain a particular local character, and it is part of the purpose of this essay to deal with the social and historical context which has produced clan politics as the particular Senegalese form of spoils-oriented factionalism. The historical experience of a century of electoral politics prior to independence, an experience unique in black Africa, is of great importance here. And the character of communal divisions, broadly and narrowly defined, helps to explain among other things the moral dimensions of a superficially amoral situation. Clan politics may then be interpreted not as a mere problem of party organisation (the official view), but as a reflection of the real bases of social solidarity within the Senegalese state.

There are a number of important problems in the study of this form of political factionalism, which should be mentioned here. The first of these lies in the informal character of the clan, the official disapproval to which it is at least nominally subject and the consequently rather furtive character of clan allegiances. For political actors, clan solidarity is normally held to be that of their opponents: although in dealing with the opposition, one may look to friends, protectors or clients in an identical manner. A further problem lies in the instability and shifting character of the clan group. The clan is not a political institution in any widely accepted sense: membership may change quite rapidly with political fortune, and the effective factional unit is defined by a situation of competition which depends on the availability of a prize. Hierarchical organisation within party and state means that clans at any given level seek alliances at other levels, and these alliances also tend to shift with political fortune. The clan is thus subject to powerful strains on the political ties between equals or unequals. But for all the instability of any given clan group, one cannot but remark on the overall durability of the clan as a form of political organisation – denounced (as Cissé Dia points out) for more than fifty years, and still going strong.

Clan politics is here understood as factionalism at each level of the state and party hierarchy, and not merely as a problem in the localities (the view of central government politicians).[3] The centre also has its clan alliances and its sectional contacts with local notables, so that factionalism should properly be seen as a principle of political action within the Senegalese state. Seen in this manner, and with regard to the communal social basis of political life, the examination of clan politics may yield a positive understanding of the phenomena conventionally labelled as 'corruption' and 'nepotism'. Where these last have become general principles of political action, it will be more fruitful to see them as such, rather than as deviations from an officially proclaimed norm which is honoured above all in the breach. Corruption and nepotism correspond fairly closely to patronage and factionalism, and the stigma attached to the former pair of terms often obscures serious analysis.[4] Clans in particular may be seen as the democratic dimension of the Senegalese state, as a means for local notables (and indirectly their followers) to assert claims on the governing elite. Possible access to patronage in this manner helps to explain the otherwise surprisingly docile attitude of peasants in the face of bureaucratic exploitation. Some peasants do benefit substantially from government handouts, under or over the counter, especially through the intermediary Muslim saint. It is also the case that handouts go above all to those geographical areas from which the government extracts most revenue (the peanut zone), a weighted proportional allocation with its own standards of equity.[5] But of course it would be very wrong to attempt to idealise such a situation: clan politics provide an accurate reflection of the social and economic inequalities which exist within the Senegalese state, inequalities within and between the communities which make up Senegalese society. In reflecting such inequalities, factionalism certainly tends to their preservation: it also (as will be argued) does much to reinforce the fragile political institutions of the Senegalese state.

COMMUNITIES

Patrons and clients, operating in groups and with shifting alliances, are the stuff of Senegalese politics. This implies that social inequalities are expressed in political terms primarily in competing alliances, each of which draws recruits from several levels in the hierarchy of power, wealth, and prestige. No analysis of 'class' tendencies in Senegalese society, such as is sketched in the previous essay, can afford to disregard this major political fact. The Wolof peasants do indeed have definable economic interests which set them at odds with the Senegalese state, but in political terms it remains crucial that the Wolof are not united, and that they are not alone among Senegal's tribal groups. Segmentary conflict at present appears stronger than nascent class antagonism. The argument here is that segmentary conflict cannot be fully understood in patron-client terms, but must be seen against a background which includes the broader bases of social differentiation in Senegal. Clientelism at a political level works within a context of social communalism. An extension of this argument is that the particular character of political clientelism in Senegal is in some measure shaped by the character of community divisions within that state. This will be argued in several ways: but in the 'class' perspective it should be noted that in this case one does not find any significant tendency for class and community boundaries to coincide – politically a most explosive combination in all post-colonial states.

A study of communal allegiances is politically crucial firstly in that it establishes the boundaries of subjective identification within Senegalese society. To identify these boundaries as 'subjective' is not to argue that they are in any sense illusory, in contrast to the 'objectively' antagonistic interests of social classes. The subjective categories of community correspond to real differences and potential antagonisms, whether in political or economic terms. Several dimensions of community loyalty must be examined here – notably those of tribe, of religion, of locality – in understanding the plural or poly-communal character of Senegalese society. Each of these dimensions is relevant to the Senegalese citizen in his response to the fundamental question – who are my people? And if the answers to this question may still to some appear illusory in the light of emerging class divisions, it can only be said that this is one illusion which can lay claim to universality. It is characteristic of Senegal, as of other post-colonial states in Africa, that the boundaries of the state do not as yet coincide with those of national identity. But it shall also be argued that the elements of a 'Senegalese' consciousness are present within the multiplicity of communal allegiances, and that it may indeed be the partial reality of Senegalese nationhood which makes possible the full efflorescence of communally-inspired clan politics.

The linguistic and cultural groupings which are labelled as 'tribal' ('national' being a term pre-empted by the post-colonial state), are of course of primary significance among communal affiliations. The sense of a shared history, in pre-colonial and colonial times, may reinforce communal solidarity. But the elementary fact is that tribesmen in the rural areas speak the language of their own tribe and are seldom proficient in any other tongue: linguistic barriers necessarily inhibit contacts (let alone a sense of mutual solidarity) between such groups. The Senegalese census of 1960–1 distinguished seven major tribal categories[6] (population over 100,000), together with nine minor ones (Table A). Such communal diversity of course has its roots in pre-colonial history, when several of the major tribes (in varying degrees) had the rudiments of a centralising institutional structure, and when inter-tribal contacts were often antagonistic and military in character. But it is important to stress the manner in which colonial rule not only increased (pacific) contact between these groups, but also developed new forms of inequality between them. Commercial agriculture, urbanisation, French education, improved communications, all these dimensions of colonial change promoted new forms of tribal inequality in general, and in specific terms especially worked to the advantage of the Wolof tribe.

The Wolof being by far the largest of Senegal's tribes (probably nearing one and a half million in 1973), have of course been fortunate in occupying both the littoral where the colonial government established the major governmental and commercial centres, and a large part of that zone of the interior which was accessible to the rail and suitable for peanut farming.[7] The Wolof in these circumstances got ahead in economic terms. They were furthermore the beneficiaries of a favourable colonial stereotype, being regarded by the French as 'reliable' and 'co-operative' as well as 'intelligent', so that they tended to be recruited preferentially to the colonial administration.[8] With the extension of structures of elective representation after 1945, and with the promotion of Africans to the higher administrative levels, the Wolof again gained. These last gains, in terms of

*TABLE A. *Principal tribes in Senegal, population 1960–1 (estimate)*

		% of total
Wolof	1,116,000	36
Serer	431,000	13.9
Fulani	356,000	11.5
Tukulor	310,000	10.0
Diola	214,000	6.9
Mandinka	146,000	4.7
Bambara	127,000	4.1
Lebu	56,000	1.8
Other	300,000	(11.1)*
	3,056,000	100.0

* Including non-African.

SOURCE: Senegalese official population estimate, results published in United States Army, *Area Handbook for Senegal*, Washington D.C., 1963, p. 62. Though one can only speculate as to the reasons for the American Army's interest in Senegal, one must recognise the value of this Handbook – the most thorough overall study of Senegal available in the English language, and remarkably reliable.

political power and influence, were of course directly those of the elite, but (as already suggested) with the trickle-down effect of patronage structures there were gains even for some Wolof peasants.

Since French conquest the Wolof have indeed become so (relatively) dominant, both in the market economy and in politics, as to occupy something of a position of cultural hegemony in Senegal. Wolof is now the *lingua franca* of trade, spoken by the great majority of town dwellers and in varying degrees familiar to an estimated two thirds of Senegal's total population.[9] There has been, especially in the coastal towns, a tendency to the 'Wolofisation' of other tribesmen – who find it attractive or expedient to adopt the Wolof language and culture as their own. And Wolof dominance now penetrates within the institutions of the dominant party and the state, despite efforts to ensure at least the public appearance of a tribal balance at the top.

A second dimension of communal identification, arguably as important in Senegal as tribal categories, is that of religion. The great majority of Senegalese (four-fifths or more) are of course Muslims, with a small Catholic minority and a substantial pagan one (Table B). Muslims are in turn divided by their adherence to the three large Sufi brotherhoods which between them account for almost the totality (97%) of Senegalese Islam. The political significance of membership in a brotherhood has been buttressed by the practice of successive Senegalese governments (colonial and independent) in using Muslim leaders as the effective indirect agents of rural administration. Brotherhood loyalties, as well as adherence to Roman Catholic or pagan beliefs, may again correspond to certain differences in economic success and political influence. While Mourides tend to be concentrated at the lower levels of the urban occupational hierarchy, largely due to their resistance to 'French' education, Catholics for the opposite reason do well.[10] Inter-denominational animosities, notably directed against Mourides (and Catholics), do exist and can become politically significant. But it is above all crucial that religious loyalties and boundaries, although sometimes overlapping with tribal ones, do on the whole tend to follow a rather different pattern. Thus although nine-tenths of Mourides are Wolof, the Wolof are in the majority of Tijani affiliation: and although nine-tenths of Tukulor are Tijani, the

Tukulor remain a minority in this latter brotherhood.[11] This pattern of cross-cutting allegiances helps to reduce the explosive potential of particular communal groups or ties.

TABLE B. *Religion in Senegal. 1960–1 (estimate)*

	Population	% of total	
Tijãniyya	1,400,000	(57+)	
Qādiriyya	415,000	(17)	
Mourides	575,000	(23+)	
Other Muslim	60,000	(2+)	
Total Muslim	2,500,000	(100)	78.5
Roman Catholic	107,000		3.5*
Traditional	540,000		18.0†

* Including Europeans and Lebanese.
† Probably over estimated.

SOURCE: U.S. Army . . . *op. cit.* p. 181.

The third significant dimension of Senegalese communalism is that of allegiance to regional or local groups. Some of the significant local groups have a basis in pre-colonial political structures, as for example in the case of the individual states formed within the Wolof cultural zone. (Kayor, Jolof, Walo, Baol and Saloum.) Although these states were suppressed and dismantled under French colonial rule, loyalty to each given area persists even with the continuing absence of political institutions at the old state level. Other powerful localisms must be seen as the direct outcome of colonial rule: thus the multi-tribal Casamance area in southern Senegal came to develop a sense of its common existence as the French administrative *Cercle* of Ziguinchor. And a sense of identification with particular colonial towns (St Louis, notably) is equally of course a product of colonial history. Local identifications become the potential basis of political animosity when one takes into account the substantial economic differences which obtain between regions (Table C). Thus government statistics suggest for example that *per capita* income is 50% higher in the Region of Sine-Saloum than in that of Casamance. Relative prosperity in rural areas has tended to coincide with the degree of involvement in commercial (peanut) agriculture: subsistence farming and pastoral zones are poorer not only by reason of their meagre production, but also in consequence of the preferential allocation of government revenue (colonial and post-colonial) to the peanut zone.[12] A sense of grievance, even of partial exclusion from the Senegalese political system, has developed in the most disadvantaged regions: in Casamance and Oriental province, for example, the people talk of a trip to the northern and western areas as 'going to Senegal'. The sense of regional (or local) loyalty has provided some effective mass basis for opposition parties and groups. Thus the left-wing *Parti du Regroupement Africain* drew much of its support from Casamance, while the Marxist-Leninist *Parti Africain de l'Indépendance* had some success in Oriental Senegal and a more substantial success in the town of St Louis (at the end of the nineteen-fifties, the time of the transfer of Senegal's capital from that town to Dakar).[13]

A tendency to the communal fragmentation of the Senegalese state may appear to be implicit in the plural nature of Senegalese society. Senegal, like other post-colonial states in Africa, suffers difficulties in the construction of an effective framework of political institutions, and this in a context where 'national' loyalties are present in widely varying degrees among the communities under the state's control. With the economic stagnation and decline of the post-independence decade, one might perhaps have expected communal bitterness to become more marked. Any such tendency to fragmentation has however to date been quite

TABLE C. *Regional population (1960–1) and average per capita income (1965), Senegal*

	Population (thousands)	Income (including a value of subsistence produce, thousands of francs CFA)
Cap-Vert	397	–
Casamance	529	13
Diourbel	502	14.4
Fleuve	342	18.1
Oriental	151	16.0
Sine-Saloum	722	20.5
Thiès	406	18.0

SOURCES: L. Verrière, 'La Population du Sénégal', Université de Dakar, *Thèse de doctorat*, 1965, p. 73, and République du Sénégal, Conseil Economique et Social, 'Note sur la Situation Agricole du Sénégal', Dakar, 1966, Annexe No. 31 (both sources unpublished).

effectively contained, and to understand this relative success it is important to consider firstly some of the particular features of Senegalese pluralism, and secondly – in greater detail – some of the features of the Senegalese style of political factionalism – clan politics. The argument will be that social structure and political style are significantly interrelated.

One important feature of Senegalese pluralism has already been touched upon, the tendency for the dimensions of communal loyalty to cut in different directions. The three crucial dimensions of particularism – tribal, religious, and local – have not been mutually reinforcing in any significant case, the tendency being for one dimension at least to cut across the other two.

The fissile potential of particularism in these circumstances has been reduced: this is clear in principle, but it is also apparently effective in fact. A second, and critically important, characteristic of Senegal's plural society concerns the character of the dominant local tribe, the Wolof. Senegal's urban culture, that of one fifth of the population, is essentially a Wolof culture. Urban migrants of other tribal groups, within a quite short space of time, may come to be considered by themselves and others as Wolof. Wolof dominance is the less resented where membership of the tribe is effectively so open: indeed it may be said that the Wolof have very successfully practised an assimilation policy on a mass basis where the French never succeeded. The practice of the French colonial administration, which never institutionalised and reinforced tribal loyalties (as did the British elsewhere in Africa), must have been important in maintaining relatively open cultural boundaries. The third notable feature of Senegal's pluralism is the unquestioned dominance of a Muslim majority whose internal divisions are contained within a shared commitment to Islam. Disputes do indeed arise between brotherhoods, or segments of brotherhoods, but the disputants themselves characteristically emphasise that 'We are all Muslims, one Book, one Prophet.' There is thus a shared commitment to an over-arching religious ideology on the part of four-fifths of the country's people, despite differences of brotherhood prayers and saintly heroes, and this commitment also may help to explain the relatively non-antagonistic character of Senegal's communal divisions.

CLANS AND CLIENTELES

The non-antagonistic nature of broad communal divisions

is important in the social background of political struggle, providing some basis for the construction of a viable Senegalese national polity. But it should also be borne in mind that 'politics' within the framework of the state and the governing party remains essentially an activity of the elite, principally of literate urban dwellers and their rural agents and intermediaries. In the context of political intrigue within the elite, it is crucial that communal segmentation – although very important – tends to the division and subdivision of broad social categories. Thus the tribal identification in politics for example is less significant than identification with a more or less extended family grouping (in certain cases, a true anthropologist's 'clan' claiming common descent from a revered ancestor).[14] Identification with a Muslim brotherhood subdivides into local lodges (or clusters of lodges), nominally teaching centres but in practice also centres of social and economic power. Regional identification breaks down to smaller localities, even to small towns and administrative units (*préfectures*, for example). Political identity of course can shift with changes in the situation and the case at issue, and loyalties to sub-units do not preclude others to larger groups. This is the logic of segmentary politics, perhaps indeed of politics in general: but it remains notable in Senegal that the 'larger' loyalties have been mobilised on few enough occasions.[15]

Communal division and subdivision help to explain the manner in which political factions perceive their divergent interests. But they do not by any means fully explain the solidarity which obtains within a given faction. These factions are each composed of patrons and their clients, and the inherent inequality of the patron-client relationship demands an understanding of the politically relevant forms of inequality. Pre-colonial forms of social and political inequality are certainly of some importance here: the hierarchy of classes and castes among the Wolof, for example, lingers on despite the disappearance of its pre-colonial economic rationale.[16] Modern political leaders, although often of humble traditional origins, seek to present themselves as traditional aristocrats. The dependence of the Muslim disciple upon his saint can also be an element in binding together a political group. The most relevant inequalities, in political terms, are also often those which have been generated by the colonial situation. Success in the market economy, as a trader or a large-scale farmer, for example, provides wealth which can be used to purchase a political following. Acquisition of some of the skills provided by French-language education is a precondition to employment at the higher levels of the state bureaucracy or the principal private businesses:[17] these positions also bring wealth and power which may be valuable in political intrigue.

Inequalities in social prestige, in wealth, and in acquired skill are each of some significance in the establishment of relations of political dependency. But the major inequality in political terms can also be seen as a broader one, that between the countryside and the town. Wealth and power are concentrated in the urban areas, especially in the capital city of Dakar – which has long been a strong centre of attraction for rural migrants. Senegal's urban dwellers (those who live in concentrations of ten thousand inhabitants and over) should now account for well over one fifth of total population: and of these, more than half live in Dakar (Table D). The 1961 Survey Census predicted a tripling of urban population within thirty years, while rural population growth over the same period would less than double. Much of the urban growth would be the product of rural-urban migration, a forecast which now appears only too well justified with the continuing stagnation of Senegal's rural economy. Official income estimates show urban employment to be very much more remunerative than any form of agriculture:

and even the urban 'unemployed', those without fixed occupation, may well be better off than most peasants.[18]

TABLE D. *Urbanisation in Senegal (1960–1) estimate*

Total urban population (population 10,000)	686,600
Total rural population	2,423,400
Urban as % total population	22.1%

Towns over 30,000 population, total populations in thousands

Dakar	374
Rufisque-Bargny	50
Kaolack	70
Thiès	69
St Louis	49

Estimated urban growth (from 1960–1), 200% in 30 years
Estimated rural growth (from 1960–1), 80% in 30 years

SOURCE: L. Verrière, *op. cit.* p. 40.

The political significance of this economic disparity between town and country lies partly in the rural-urban hostilities which have on occasion been successfully exploited by agile politicians. Leopold Senghor's decisive electoral victories in 1951 and 1952 were in considerable measure due to his appeal as the 'peasant's candidate' against the corrupt urban faction of Lamine Guèye. But these are transient events: Senghor in power meant the dominance of a party effectively as urban (and as corrupt) as Lamine Guèye's S.F.I.O. The stable situation remains one in which political (and economic) power radiates out from the capital city to the regional centres, and then to the countryside. Factional politics is above all a matter for urban activists, who do indeed seek alliances with rural notables: but power within such alliances remains weighted on the side of urban bureaucrats or party functionaries. The centralisation of the peanut trade under government control since independence has eliminated many regional centres of private trading, wealth and power. Government expenditure is almost all allocated from the centre: there is no institutionalised local control over the amounts involved, although some influence remains over the specific use of funds. The state, centralised at Dakar, now effectively holds the purse-strings for the entire territory of Senegal.

The predicament of the rural people of Senegal, and in particular of the peasants who produce the majority of the country's wealth, is thus in political terms one of weakness, internal division, and dependence. Peasants are indeed exploited as a socio-economic category, while they remain marginal (or sometimes indeed apparently irrelevant) to the political operation of the state to which they are subject. But it is also the case that the workings of patron-client politics do permit a minority even of peasants to gain in determinate ways if they give their support to a local leader with influential connections in the city. Any nascent sense of class solidarity among peasants is thus at odds not only with broad communal divisions and relative inequalities, but also with clan political clientelism.

Political competition within the Senegalese elite has already been referred to as a spoils system. The alliances and groups which form in such competition are directed firstly to jobs and secondly to the material benefits which may accrue to the job-holder and his following. Such alliances are inherently unstable, lacking as they do an institutional coherence such as is provided by a political party, or a shared ideological commitment in any broad sense. The patron-client bond at an elite level, more specifically, appears to be a temporary and flimsy one. Where a given aspirant patron achieves his goal, a post of power and influence, and can thus accord other positions to his clients, the political clan begins to disperse. Those clients who have been rewarded soon lose their sense of gratitude, while the unrewarded ones soon have to seek another patron.[19]

With the necessarily extreme instability of a political group directed purely to a spoils goal, it is not surprising that the more durable and successful political teams are in fact bound together by other ties. There must at the least be sufficient moral sanction on clan members to inhibit acts of political treachery, to provide a minimal basis of predictability and mutual trust. And in the fragmented social and political structure of Senegal, it is predictable that the effective basis of political trust should to a large extent reflect communal divisions: the trustworthy are one's relatives, one's co-believers, those who share one's local origins ('home-boys'). These bonds are the more effective when (as is frequently the case) they are combined. And they can be reinforced by past experience of reciprocal exchange of favours in politics or business. This obtains for alliances either of equals or unequals: a sense of shared interest is complemented by other shared values. Thus a system which may readily be stigmatised as corrupt is not without its ethical element: in Senegal as elsewhere, there is a morality of corruption.

Clan politics as a system in Senegal – and the practice of factionalism does exhibit sufficient regularities to merit the label of 'system' – has emerged from a local historical tradition of electoral institutions which goes back to the middle of the last century. This unique electoral tradition has been of great significance in establishing some of the local rules on the manner in which factional struggle is carried on – in forming a local style of politics which has lasted to the present day – and also in training an elite with a reservoir of skills in the arts of politics. The historical experience of politics in the four coastal *communes* of Senegal is thus too important to be passed over in an analysis of modern politics, although no more can be done here than to indicate a few salient features of the commune tradition.[20]

The French revolution of 1848 gave the colony of Senegal (then confined to the coastal settlements of Gorée and St Louis) the right to elect a deputy to the French National Assembly. The right was withdrawn under Napoleon III, but restored definitively in 1871. Elected municipal councils were established in the latter part of the nineteenth century, first at Gorée and St Louis, later at Dakar and Rufisque. A colonial assembly was created in 1879 with responsibility for the communes as a whole.

The great majority of the commune electorate was African, universal male suffrage being observed from the outset, although French and mulatto (*métis*) representatives were dominant until 1914. The election of an African deputy (Blaise Diagne) in that year ended the dominance of the French and mulattos among elected representatives: the poor and illiterate African electorate may often (realistically enough) have remained unmoved by the political programmes advanced by candidates, but they did react to their skin colour. The election of African representatives did not however guarantee African political dominance, and commune politics effectively remained a 'rotten borough' tradition dominated by the money of French and mulatto traders and by the bureaucratic weight of the French colonial administration.

Blaise Diagne, who remained Deputy for Senegal from 1914 until his death in 1934, was the master practitioner of these politics of dependency. He did indeed serve the interests of the Bordeaux traders who dominated the commercial life of Senegal, services recognised when he was buried with due ceremony in Bordeaux. He also served the interests of the colonial government, for whom he helped to recruit thousands of African soldiers in the first world war and on whose behalf he defended the practice of forced labour in France's colonies before the International Labour Conference at Geneva in 1930. But he did prove adept in building for himself a position of considerable personal political power: the political connections which he established in Paris made him feared, and in some cases hated, by local colonial officials. A local newspaper of 1932, reporting on one of Diagne's election rallies at St Louis, gives some suggestion of the motives for the resentment of colonial officials and the admiration of black citizens: 'It was a royal comedy for the natives to watch the highest administrators advance in turn to make a bow . . . M. Diagne, impassive, with his haughty and arrogant air, received the respects due to his eminent position. Meanwhile a praise-singer sang in Tukulor – "Here is the king of the white men."' [21] One Governor General resigned rather than collaborate with him (Van Vollenhoven, in 1918). One Governor of Senegal (Beurnier, 1930–6) publicly recognised that he owed his appointment in large part to Diagne. Another senior official referred to Diagne's style, in a pencilled note on an administrative report, as 'fundamentally dishonest' (*foncièrement improbe*). The same note did also recognise a certain grandeur in this style of corruption, which was contrasted to that of Senegal's other 'little politicians'.[22] Diagne did have considerable influence in the dispensation of administrative and political patronage, which he used to build a powerful local political machine: he also used his influence on many occasions to favour his native *commune* of Gorée. His skill in the political arts, and in particular in the arts of exploiting a dependent position to his own advantage, make him a true precursor of the man who has dominated Senegalese politics since 1951, Leopold Senghor. While Senghor was a student in Paris, Diagne acted as his legal guardian and apparently initiated him to the arts of politics. Subsequent history shows that the young Senghor must have learned these lessons well.

The colony's deputy, with his connections and influence in Paris, controlled the major patronage resources, including money from the major companies and even many administrative job appointments. Other local politicians were basically concerned with the patronage dispensed by the municipal councils: this was above all a matter of jobs, a plethoric employment of friends and dependents in posts which were often effectively sinecures. An official report of a meeting of the St Louis Municipal Council, in 1946, suggests something of the flavour of politics at this level:

> The Mayor declares that the question of municipal personnel is very important, and informs the Council that among municipal employees some are favoured at the expense of others.
>
> El Hadj Maxa Sène takes note of the fact that the inhabitants of Guet Ndar [neighbourhood] have no jobs in the municipality.
>
> Khayar Mbèngue feels that we must think of our old friends, to bring them back to the municipality, and feels that the council should turn to the case of our friends Doudou Siby, Charles Assa, Sidi Faye and Abou Diakhaté, all very devoted to the party.
>
> Maxa Sène agrees that these cases are interesting, but reproaches the Council with concerning itself solely with braggarts, completely neglecting the more interesting case of the Guet Ndarians who bring more votes to the party than those people . . .
>
> Ngay Fall insists that we must continue to the end our battle to place our friends.[23]

This last declaration of intent is in the true idiom of Senegal's clan politics.

The colonial administration over the inter-war years (notably by the *Arrêté* No. 3361 of 1928) assumed many of the municipal functions which the elected authorities discharged either inadequately or not at all. In 1941, an estimated 75% of the municipal budget of St Louis went on jobs alone, and the struggle to place one's clients remained the core of municipal politics.[24] Municipal funds could be privately appropriated, and subsidies collected from the local trading companies (not, in general, from the major Bordeaux interests which could afford to remain aloof from this petty strife).

Electoral contests in the communes were occasions for a wide range of political malpractices. Results could in some instances simply be falsely declared by the colonial administration, as was certainly the case in the re-election of Blaise Diagne in 1928.[25] They were more frequently influenced by the money and goods distributed at election time, resources which in large part originated with the trading companies. And they were always influenced by the fraudulent distribution of citizenship certificates (based on birth supposedly within Commune boundaries) to supporters.[26] Those already entrenched in office usually had the advantage over their opponents in these practices, so that power once achieved in Commune politics was characteristically self-perpetuating.

The political alignments which contested these elections were the ancestors of the modern Senegalese political clan. Electoral propaganda was above all concentrated on stylised personal abuse: thus Diagne in the 1932 election was variously described by his opponents as a 'vampire' an 'ex-houseboy' and a '*petit nègre*'.[27] Personal attacks could be complemented by communal abuse, as when Lamine Guèye's supporters in 1938 described their opponents as 'a majority of contemptible Lebu' (tribe in the Dakar area) and 'a few unwashed St Louisians'.[28] But the prevalent tendency was to dwell on the moral and other faults of the opposition rather than on one's own virtues or programmes. In electoral politics, this may often be the only plausible approach for a candidate to adopt: certainly the tendency has no uniquely Senegalese character. At the same time it is true that a survey of the Senegalese political press for the period 1914–40 reveals a remarkably low salience of broad policy issues.[29]

The personality-centred factions of the communes did indeed frequently present themselves in the guise of political parties, but the ideological divergences which they flaunted on occasion were imported from France – and in particular from the metropolitan political party to which they were affiliated and from which they drew their subsidies. Thus the Socialist Lamine Guèye might refer to his opponents as 'Fascits', while he himself was called by Galandou Diouf a 'Communist and freemason':[30] but few if any Senegalese took this sort of talk very seriously. Galandou Diouf, before he became publicly preoccupied with communism and freemasonry under the Vichy régime, summed up the policy content of commune electoral appeals in his oppositional slogan – 'Everything that is against Diagne is Ours.'[31]

Reforms introduced by the French government in 1945 ended the restriction of the franchise to the coastal communes, and the electoral balance thereafter rapidly shifted in favour of the rural areas. Senghor's early electoral triumphs have often (and in part correctly)[32] been ascribed to his recognition of this elementary political fact. But the legacy of the commune tradition remained very important, notably so in terms of political skills and style. A class of professional politicians had emerged in the communes; the literate intermediaries like Mody Mbaye who made their living by writing letters to senior colonial officials on behalf of illiterate clients, enabling these clients to register complaints against the corrupt or arbitrary actions of local administrative agents; businessmen like Galandou Diouf (Deputy 1934–41) with a political clientele in part composed of their commercial debtors; lawyers like Lamine

Guèye, supported by the Lebu in Dakar because he acted in land cases for the Lebu chiefs against the colonial administration; even the university lecturer Leopold Senghor, who learned all he needed to know at the feet of the master, Blaise Diagne. These were men who had learned a trick or two in politics, and they provided Senegal with an important legacy for the post-war years: the legacy was one of political skill, 'corrupt' and 'nepotistical' certainly, but also highly complex and adroit.

Senghor's political party, originally (1948–56) named the *Bloc Démocratique Sénégalais*, formally repudiated the corruption and misgovernment of the commune tradition. But the party's leaders have frequently recognised the extent to which their own internal organisation remains influenced by that tradition. Already in 1950, Senghor publicly complained at a party conference that 'many comrades remain nepotists', while seventeen years later the Minister of the Interior indulged in a remarkable display of breast-beating at the annual party conference: 'the permanent institutions of the party are non-existent, or when they exist, they are skeletal, inoperative and ineffective.[33] Effective party organisation, in the dominant party and its opponents, has relied less on formal structures than on informal patron-client factionalism. The assimilation of opposition parties within Senghor's *Union Progressiste Sénégalaise* merely gives an added complexity to the clan divisions.[34] And the frequent public and private campaigns to eliminate corruption and factionalism, although they do perhaps reflect some real concern at least on the part of President Senghor, tend to be applied selectively to the detriment of particular individuals and clans and to the advantage of others.

Senegal's independence in 1960 meant the transfer of the state's administrative powers from the French colonial rulers to the political leaders of the dominant parties: and since independence, despite the continuing presence and administrative influence of French personnel,[35] Africans have come to hold the majority of important posts both at the centre and in the localities. There is thus at present in principle a parallel hierarchy of government, with distinct party and state institutions at each administrative level: state capital, regional centre, department. In practice the state administration has been dominant, but it has also become inextricably involved in party politics – and particularly in the factional struggles within the *Union Progressiste Sénégalaise*. The practical consequences of this trend, in the context of local administration, were noted by a semi-official report of 1964:

> the interference of politicians in the working of regional administration is constant. Any civil servant who desires to fulfil his administrative duties while standing aside from political intrigue rapidly discovers that this is impossible. Either he must resign himself to semi-inactivity, or he must commit himself politically to preserve his chances of working. Unfortunately, local politics is all too seldom based on ideology, but remains a struggle of clans and personal influence. It is based not on militants but on a clientele. Caught in a trap, the civil servant becomes a clan man.[36]

The observation is accurate enough, if one ignores the curious Gallic preference for ideological political struggle. Not all civil servants, however, are dismayed or surprised by these facts of political life, and clan connections are valued not only as a means to 'get the job done' but also as a path to career success. Administrators at local, regional and national levels cultivate their political connections, and may also develop contacts in the world of private business with a view to illicit financial gain. The increasing dominance of the state administration over the party since independence has thus led not to a victory of impersonal bureaucracy over political factionalism, rather the contrary. And this implies that the basic situation of dominance of the state in the rural economy, with the bureaucratic exploitation of peasants which it has involved, has been greatly complicated by internal factionalism within the dominant 'class': the situation then becomes all the more complex when one takes account of the clientele links between particular factions of notables and their particular mass followings.

The clientele dimension of clan politics thus introduces the problems of the connection between the minority of urban activists and the massive rural majority of Senegalese citizens: this is a dimension which will be interpreted as being, in a peculiar and narrowly selective sense, democratic. The politically influential, and aspirants to influence, have all since 1945 been concerned to some degree with the building of a mass following, although their reasons for doing so have evolved over time. One reason alone had been sufficient in the pre-1945 urban politics of the Communes – the votes of illiterate citizens. In the decade following the second world war the competing political parties each sought to win peasant votes. Those individual leaders and factions who could claim the allegiance of voters in a particular area were in a position to claim a corresponding prominence within party organisations. Electoral competition reached its height in the nineteen-fifties, and in rural Senegal this was the heyday of the saints of the Muslim brotherhoods, who delivered their followers to the polls in support of one or other urban politician.[37] It was also the time of the downfall of the colonial canton chiefs, resentment of whom was skilfully exploited by Senghor's party. Absorption of the opposition within the governing party since independence, and the control exercised by the government on the declaration of election results, have deprived the vote of much of its significance: since 1966 there has been no legal opposition party in Senegal.

Elections do nonetheless still take place at each level (region, department, municipality) within the single-party structure, and there is a measure of real competition for party office between factions at each of these levels. The eligible electorate is made up of party members, those who have purchased a party card: this gives rise to a series of malpractices which make the U.P.S. card the modern equivalent of the certificate of commune citizenship. Competing clans seek to distribute a maximum of these cards to their supporters, and where possible to deny them to their opponents (this becomes possible where the clan concerned has secured control of the local party machinery). Cards may be sold on a more or less compulsory basis through local notables at regional, department or *section* levels: this has been a historic practice in the agricultural credit organisations, *Sociétés de Prévoyance* and Co-operatives, where the distribution of credit has often been subject to the prior distribution of party cards. The notable distributing the cards may then be in a position to make a block vote in the names of those to whom cards have been sold. A simplified procedure, the occasion of some official enquiries, is for the notable concerned to purchase the cards himself in the names of real or putative supporters: this practice is restricted principally by the finances available to party officers. The party leader for the Region of Thiès, for example, was believed in 1967 to have many thousands of such cards (ostensibly sold) in his personal possession, for use on appropriate occasions. However the cards are distributed, and there are many who adhere to the party on a genuinely voluntary basis, it is membership support which in large part defines the prestige and power of party notables.[38] The operation of clan politics as a political system assumes that the government is made up of a number of factions, politically weighted by the extent of their support in each case: the national government can then be seen as an aggregation of clans which together account for a majority at least of those actively concerned with politics.

Electoral support, given the prevalent abuses within the U.P.S., is not of course an adequate basis for the measurement of influence in real terms. Political leaders at the national level make their own calculations of the local influences of given clans, and the central leadership (President Senghor in particular) plays astutely on local rivalries in maintaining control. The governing principle in the regions and localities, where the President is concerned, appears to be that one never seeks to discipline any local clan without giving corresponding support to its major rival in the same local area. The central government must be concerned with its overall support on a national basis, and minimally must assure that it stays in power, that it preserves public order, and that it secures compliance in matters of taxation and other government levies. Effective opposition to the government has tended to draw support from the left-wing groups of urban areas: the government needs rural support to counter-balance the urban militants. And this in turn means that despite the steady flow of official rhetoric against the clan tendency within the party and government, Senghor is in practical terms committed to the maintenance of a factional politics which rests on existing local power and influence. After the anti-government riots of workers and students in Dakar in 1968, prefects across the country received a circular letter which instructed them to 'respond to requests from local clan leaders for administrative patronage'.[39]

The control which the central government now effectively maintains over local expenditure makes it possible to manipulate this administrative patronage very effectively in building political support. Roads, deep wells, schools, dispensaries, land grants, are allocated above all to those areas where a powerful faction exists with good connections in governing circles in Dakar. Agricultural credit, and even the distribution of food (millet and rice) in the pre-harvest hungry season are subject to the same politically selective principles. All of this represents a tradition established under colonial rule, when the French administration was very much concerned to reward those local faction leaders who could promise the support of their clients, and correspondingly to punish those faction leaders who seemed hostile to the French interest. The situation has however become more complex since independence, as the central government is now itself factionally divided. The local faction or clan must now seek to establish relations with other clans at higher levels, and those who lose out in a local struggle may still redeem their situation by an astute calculation of a changing balance of power at the centre.

Rural notables, clan leaders in contemporary terms, are as indispensable to the present government of Senegal as they were in the past to the colonial administration: and they are indispensable intermediaries for what is essentially the same reason in each case, the inadequacy of formal institutions in organising support at a mass level. The saints of the Muslim brotherhoods in this context remain the principal actors: the leading saints are in a position to demand many favours, as they do in general remain the popularly recognised authorities in rural Senegal. A French administrator noted this with reference to elections in the nineteen-fifties: 'in most cases, one must admit that in the mind of the bush voter, these electoral contests are at best confused and that when the time comes he will leave the choice to his *marabout*.'[40] The observation is accurate, and remains relevant to the largely non-electoral clan politics of today. But any imputation of a blind religious deference, such as Quesnot on the whole suggests, would be mistaken. Peasants do benefit from the political patronage which their holy men can procure, and saints with good political connections recruit new followers on this basis. The mechanism is thus self-reinforcing. Government leaders see that preferential access to administrative favours is given to those saints who are deemed to have a large body of disciples, and the saints then use this patronage to recruit more disciples. The peasants who 'leave politics to their *marabouts*' are thus in effect making a very rational decision, as long as the allocation of government expenditure in rural areas follows such a pattern of political influence. Two examples among many may at least suggest the efficacy of saintly politics: in one case a saint, whose village bordered on Senegal's central desert, secured the installation of no less than four diesel-pumped deep wells there, at a total cost to the state of £100,000; in another case, a saint procured an eleven-mile extension of a tarred road terminating in his own village and at his front door.

Followers as well as leaders benefit from such official favours: without religious leadership and organisation, peasants in all likelihood would simply be helpless victims of government exactions. The hostility of rural people to the state and its urban controllers is thus tempered by the hope that they may be among the lucky ones if their local patron plays his cards right. Where this hope is consistently disappointed, in the last resort they may (and do) change their allegiance to a more favourably placed local leader: no saint can afford a record of failure in his intrigues with the national or local government authorities. The Senegalese tradition of clan politics, as it functions in the rural areas, thus provides an effective channel for patronage redistribution from the centre to the localities. The existence of such structures of patronage politics, parallel with the formal (bureaucratic) institutions of state administration, serves both to soften the exploitative features of the state in rural areas, and (partially in consequence) to provide some of the basis for a viable polity in Senegal.

CONCLUSION

Clan politics has been described here as a variety of moral system if understood in its own terms, a network of reciprocal exchange in which notions (even misguided) of mutual trust and obligation have an important place. To conclude this essay it seems necessary for the author to present certain of his own judgments. An author's normative view will be present even where it is not made explicit, and there are many good reasons to make it explicit – of which the first and sufficient reason in this case is to avoid appearing (if only by omission) simply to endorse the morality of Senegal's clan politicians. The relevant areas of enquiry, then, to be treated here, are the economic consequences of the operation of this style of politics, the international context within which it operates, and the principle consequences in terms of the likely political future of Senegal.

The politics of patronage and communal representation, of a type broadly similar to that found in Senegal, have been found in other countries to involve certain costs in terms of economic development. Economic stagnation, in this view, is the price of political stability – and a price which in this sophisticated view is well worth paying.[41] Senegal is indeed economically stagnant: World Bank estimates of the country's *per capita* 'growth' rate in the 1960s are set at an annual average of –0.1%. But any 'political' explanation for this meagre performance seems of small significance when set against the harsh facts of Senegal's economic predicament: dependence on a single export crop (peanuts) the value of which has fallen fairly consistently over the past decade, paucity of alternative agricultural produce adapted to the poor soils of most of the country, virtual absence of mineral wealth, and population growth estimated at 2.5% per annum. One may strongly doubt whether any government bent on a firmer political discipline, whether that government be one of military officers or left-wing revolutionaries, could achieve substantially more than that of Senghor in the face of such a bleak economic situation. The question of 'stagnation as the price of political stability' at present simply does not arise in Senegal.

No discussion of Senegalese politics should leave out of account the problems posed by the continuing dependence of the country on the ex-colonial power: Senegal today remains in many respects one of France's neo-colonies (or, better, client states). The bulk of import and export trade is with France, governmental financial aid and private investment still come (although of late in declining quantities) from France, and the French government helps to sustain the Senegalese state by the provision of administrative and even military personnel.[42] But while all this is undoubtedly important in setting limits to the reality of Senegal's independence, it also remains the case both that political struggle within the Senegalese state is seldom directly concerned with the French, and that the French have little sustained concern with Senegal's domestic politics. French influence has acted above all through Senghor as President of the Republic: and it is true that Senegal's politicians (and also soldiers) are well aware that France has valued the continuing presence of Senghor as head of state, and that in a crisis France might intervene to protect him (as she has done in the past, in the early 1960s). This knowledge does indeed set a limit to the ambitions of clan politicians: but apart from this elementary consideration the Senegalese style of internal politics remains one of creative indigenous adaptation. And even assuming the advent of a new regime hostile to France, it could scarcely operate for long in defiance of clan political patterns. It is suggestive, in this regard, that both the left-wing – and to some degree anti-

French – parties have had considerable problems with internal factionalism (this, as government spokesmen point out with relish, while such parties were not even exposed to 'the multiple temptations of power').[43]

While clan politics appears to be little more than marginally relevant to the (important) problems of economic stagnation and external dependence, it does seem to offer a number of very significant advantages in building a polity equipped to cope with the realities of Senegalese society. In the first place, modern (post-independence) clan politics represents the effective fusion of two distinct political traditions, one rural and the other urban. The historic political practices of Senegal's Communes have persisted to the present, only superficially changed, but they have now incorporated the established hierarchies of the rural hinterland – in particular, the Muslim brotherhoods. As already indicated, there is a political bridge across the urban-rural gap, and the cash does cross in both directions.

Clan politics also of course provides for existing social realities in enabling some form of representation for the various communities which make up the Senegalese state. This representation is, as already indicated, proportional in giving most political weight to those communities in rural society which are most involved in the money economy upon which the state depends, and also in favouring those communities which are most effectively organised. Representation along these lines, while perpetuating and even reinforcing communal inequalities, perhaps paradoxically gives some sense of equity which helps to contain potential communal strife. And it is in this last area that one may most clearly recognise the actual and potential achievements of clan politics. For African states in their present phase, the dangers of communal strife seem a good deal more immediate than the prospects of any revolutionary political solution which could render communal inequalities irrelevant by a rigorous political discipline imposed from the centre. The haunting example of the recent history of Nigeria indeed suggests that any such attempt to override communal realities is likely to be illusory in that it will act effectively to the immediate benefit of those communities best represented in the central government, and thus provoke hostilities in excluded communities with an outcome in violence and destruction.

Senegal at present (1973) appears to have a good chance of avoiding such a human disaster. Not only have communal antagonisms been quite effectively contained within the framework of clan competition, but there has been an emergence of some sense of a Senegalese national identity. This identity centres around the capital city of Dakar, around the governing elite, and also (importantly) around the personality of the head of state. The political skill of President Senghor is certainly not a negligible factor in the relative stability which Senegal has enjoyed since independence: his status as member of a minority tribe (Serer), and a minority religion (Catholic) appears to make him an acceptable mediator for the larger communities. It is true of course that a 'Senegalese' identity has developed in widely varying degrees through the territory of Senegal, being strongest in the northern and western areas, weakest to the south and east. But it is again important that the Wolof tribe, dominant in the larger towns and cash-cropping areas of the north-west, are no tribal exclusivists.

To interpret Senegalese politics as a relatively viable mechanism for the reconciliation of divergent group interests should not be to ignore the extent to which it operates to the exclusion of certain individuals and groups. There are political losers in Senegal as elsewhere. Opposition parties, it is true, have in general been incorporated to the governing party rather than simply suppressed, but the use or threat of the state stick has accompanied the carrot of office. And in two important cases, those of the Marxist-Leninist *Parti Africain de l'Indépendance* (banned since 1960) and of the ex-Prime Minister Mamadou Dia (detained since 1962), the apparatus of state repression has been used by President Senghor and his colleagues to devastating effect. The government still reacts with particular decisiveness against those who oppose it while presenting themselves as being of the 'Left' (Trade Unions and students in the Dakar disorders of 1968, for example). But there are also ideological divisions, which might be broadly categorised in Left-Right terms, within the governing elite itself; and it must be said that the extra-governmental Left – urban, small and divided – scarcely at present constitutes a credible political alternative in Senegal.

This essay, in sum, has attempted a sketch of the political sociology of Senegal as a post-colonial state, of the communities which make up the state and the style of government which has evolved from the various local political traditions. The limits of Senegal's achievement have been recognised, and they are important – economic stagnation, social inequalities of various kinds which have been perpetuated or accentuated, a continuing dependence on France. But the positive achievements also deserve a full recognition. Senegal's political style may appear unedifying to some, but it has permitted social peace and the gradual emergence of a viable national state. This is indeed a largely extra-institutional model of political order, but it does appear to work.

NOTES

1 Both the above quotations are drawn from a speech by Cissé Dia, then minister of the Interior. See *Dakar-Matin*, 17 May 1967. Leopold Senghor much earlier expressed himself in similar terms: '*le népotisme est un mal Sénégalais*'. See *Condition Humaine*, 2 May 1950.

2 See R. Lemarchand and K. Legg, 'Political Clientelism and Development', in *Comparative Politics*, Vol. 4, No. 2, 1971. For a discussion of the 'spoils system', see Carl H. Landé, *Leaders, Factions, and Parties: the Structure of Philippine Politics*, Yale University, Southeast Asia Monographs, 1966. The most useful introduction to the phenomenology of political situations such as that of Senegal is Fred Riggs, *Administration in Developing Countries*, Boston: Houghton Mifflin, 1964.

3 F. Zuccarelli, in the only full-length study of the governing *Union Progressiste Sénégalaise*, on the whole endorses this view. F. Zuccarelli, *Un Parti Politique Africain*, Paris: Pichon et Durand-Auzias, 1970, p. 171 and throughout.

4 There are of course exceptions here. See Riggs, *Administration in Developing Countries* . . ., and S. Andreski, *The African Predicament*, London: Michael Joseph, 1968, for imaginative scholarly views on corruption and nepotism in new states.

5 A possible bias on my part should be recognised here, in that my research was conducted among those who did best out of this 'weighted proportional allocation' and thus had most reason to be satisfied by its 'equity'. But travel elsewhere in Senegal (including the poorer non-Wolof regions of Casamance and Fleuve) established an impression at least of popular resignation (if not satisfaction) in face of the proportionality involved.

6 Of these seven, four should linguistically be treated as two only. Fulani and Tukulor, Mandinka and Bambara, are pairs which each effectively represent a single language.

7 This zone accounts for one half of Senegal's population on one seventh of Senegal's territory. République du Sénégal, *Rapport Général sur les Perspectives de Développement du Sénégal*, Dakar, 1960, p. 1–1 (27).

8 S. Gellar, 'The Politics of Development in Senegal', Ph. D. Thesis in Politics, Columbia University, 1967, p. 12.

9 This estimate is advanced in G. Wesley Johnson, *The Emergence of Black Politics in Senegal*, Stanford: Stanford University Press, 1971, p. 9.

10 Educational differences by religion are quite significant. The Dakar census of 1955 found that among African male Christians, 76% spoke French and 55% were literate in French: comparable figures for the Tijani were 49%/33%, for Mourides 30%/15%. In *Recensement Démographique de Dakar*, (1955), Paris, 1958, Vol. I, p. 37.

11 D. Cruise O'Brien, *The Mourides* . . ., pp. 242–3, provides statistical detail.

12 On inter-regional competition for government spending, and resentment of preference given to the peanut zone, S. Gellar, 'The Politics . . . ', p. 170.
13 Prior to independence in 1960, St Louisians monopolised the best government jobs open to Africans. G. Wesley Johnson, *The Emergence* . . . , p. 36.
14 On Wolof kinship, see the sources mentioned in note 3 of the Introduction to this volume.
15 The most significant 'larger' communal loyalty probably remains that to the relatively deprived southern region of Casamance, although the political sense of regional deprivation was softened with the incorporation of Assane Seck and some of the Casamance leadership to the governing party in 1966.
16 The only study specifically on Wolof castes, to date, is O. Silla, 'Les Castes dans la Société Ouolof', *Mémoire*, Ecole Pratique des Hautes Etudes (Paris), 1965.
17 Gellar estimates that less than twenty per cent of Senegalese speak or understand French, and that little over half of that proportion are literate in the language. This proportion is of course, as already indicated, differentially distributed in communal terms. S. Gellar, 'The Politics . . . ', p. 17.
18 The disproportion between urban and rural incomes is underlined by I.R.F.E.D., 'Le Sénégal en Marche', *Les Cahiers Africains*, No. 5, 1962, p. 18.
19 This point, together with much of the background material for the analysis presented here, emerged from interviews and conversations with local politicians and civil servants in Senegal in 1966–7. The 'disintegrative' tendency of the Senegalese clan should provide food for thought for those scholars who imagine patron-client systems to be inherently self-reinforcing.
20 A valuable source on Commune politics is G. Wesley Johnson, *The Emergence of Black Politics in Senegal* . . . , although the analysis presented here is at variance with Johnson on a number of points. Specifically, I feel that Johnson has overstated and misunderstood the significance of local 'party' organisation, and that he misinterprets African politics of the period under his consideration (1900–20) in the light of nationalist movements of a much later period.
21 *L'Action Sénégalaise*, 11 June 1932. Diagne became Under-Secretary of State for the Colonies in the French cabinet in 1931.
22 On Diagne's dishonesty, 'Notice Concernant M. Galandou Diouf', in *Archives de la République du Sénégal*, Dakar (*A.R.S.D.*), 13G 17/17. On Beurnier, *Notes Africaines* (Dakar), No. 135, July 1972, p. 69.
23 *A.R.S.D.* 13G 17/36.
24 For an idea of the continuity of this tradition of plethoric sinecure employment and urban misgovernment, see *West Africa*, 29 March 1958 (on Dakar municipality in the nineteen-fifties), and C. Cottingham, 'Clan Politics and Rural Modernisation', Ph.D. Thesis, University of California Berkeley, 1969 (on Communes throughout Senegal in the nineteen-sixties). The latter source (p. 83) shows that in 1964–5, 21 out of 32 municipalities spent over 55% (and up to 80%) of their budgets on personnel alone.
25 Michel Leiris, on his travels across Africa, met a French administrator who talked jovially of his own part in these activities.' M. Leiris, *L'Afrique Fantôme*, Paris: Gallimard, 1934.
26 Accusations of this type were made by the defeated candidates in all important elections of the 1920s and 1930s.
27 *L'Action Sénégalaise*, 13 February 1932, and *L'Opposition*, 26 April 1932.

The latter newspaper also attacked Diagne as 'the man of Bordeaux'; its own candidate, Galandou Diouf, was later (after his election in 1934) to be the representative of the same French trading interests.

28 L'A.O.F., 1 January 1938.

29 The author has made a complete survey of the Senegalese press for this period, available in Paris at the *Bibliothèque Nationale*, and in Dakar at the *Institut Fondamental d'Afrique Noire*.

30 *L'A.O.F.*, 26 February 1938; *Le Périscope Africain*, 8 August 1936; *A.R.S.D.* 13G 17/17.

31 *L'Opposition*, in 1932, carried this quotation from Diouf as its masthead.

32 Senghor's triumph also owed something to political divisions within the French administration which supervised the election. On the expansion of the franchise after 1945, see K. Robinson, 'Senegal', in Robinson and W. J. M. Mackenzie (eds.), *Five Elections in Africa*, Oxford: Clarendon Press, 1960.

33 Senghor in *Condition Humaine*, 2 May 1950: Cissé Dia in *Dakar-Matin*, 17 May 1967.

34 On the absorption of the organised opposition, see D. Cruise O'Brien, 'Political Opposition in Senegal', in *Government and Opposition*, Vol. 2, No. 4, July-October 1967.

35 On this question, see Rita Cruise O'Brien, 'Colonialism to Cooperation? French Technical Assistance in Senegal', in *The Journal of Development Studies*, Vol. 8, No. 1, October 1971.

36 République du Sénégal, *Rapport de Synthèse*, Dakar: CINAM, 1964, p. 23.

37 See D. Cruise O'Brien, *The Mourides* . . . , Ch. 12, for details.

38 F. Zuccarelli, p. 126, gives figures for U.P.S. membership over the period 1961–6. He also gives a breakdown of these figures by Region, which acquires a certain importance when it is noted that places on the National Council of the U.P.S. are allocated to Regions in proportion to regional membership. Figures in 1966 were as follows (in thousands): Region of Cap Vert, 67, Casamance 79, Diourbel 54, Fleuve 40, Oriental 20, Sine-Saloum 91, Thiès 33. It should also be noted that below Department level, Party elections have always been almost totally fictitious events.

39 Cited in C. Cottingham, 'Political Consolidation and Centre-Local Relations in Senegal', in *The Canadian Journal of African Studies*, Vol. 4, No. 1, Winter 1970, p. 114.

40 F. Quesnot, 'L'Evolution du Tidjanisme Sénégalais depuis 1922', Paris, Centre de Hautes Etudes Administratives sur l'Afrique et l'Asie Modernes, *Mémoire*, No. 2865, 1958, pp. 88–9.

41 See M. Weiner (ed.), *Modernization*, New York: Basic Books, 1967, pp. 167–8. Also A. Zolberg, *Creating Political Order*, Chicago: Rand McNally, 1966, pp. 73–7.

42 These questions are thoroughly discussed in Rita Cruise O'Brien, *White Society in Black Africa. The French of Senegal*, London: Faber, 1972.

43 *Dakar-Matin*, 17 May 1967 (speech of Cissé Dia).

Conclusion: The politics of corruption

'Corruption', over the years, has emerged as Senegal's national political style. And it is a style locally worn with a certain characteristic elegance. Outsiders of all kinds (technical assistants, journalists and scholars of various nationalities) have long recognised the prevalence of the style. Their reactions, whether in the case of right-wing bureaucratic technicians or of left-wing socialist modernisers, have in general included at least an element of puritanical disgust. Those with a sense of humour have found corresponding material for their amusement in the devious Senegalese machinations, those with a sense of style have found something to admire in the sheer bravura of local political intrigue. This span of reactions applies to citizens of neighbouring African states as well as to European or American observers. To their neighbours, the Senegalese have been objects of contempt for the apparent amorality of their political life. Beneath this gratifying disdain, however, one can usually detect some reluctant admiration for the skill of Senegal's political elite. And for this writer also the reaction and the judgment remain somewhat ambivalent: before solemnly pronouncing judgment, however, I think that it is important (necessary) to disentangle the various political activities stigmatised as 'corrupt', to attempt some historical explanation of their development, and to suggest reasons for the success (at least in its own terms) of the Senegalese political style. In other words, one must attempt answers to these three questions – *How* are the Senegalese corrupt? *Why* are they corrupt? How have they come to be *so skilful* in the corrupt arts of politics?

It is perhaps most convenient to answer these questions in less than strictly logical sequence, taking the second question first. An initial answer at least is readily available here in a large body of literature on post-colonial regimes in Africa and elsewhere, and has already been suggested as at least partially applicable in several of these essays on Senegal. This would suggest that colonial rule at a formal level created only very fragile political institutions, tenuously connected from the governing centres to the governed masses (Wolof or other). If viable connections were to be established between the bureaucratic centres (Dakar, St Louis) and the illiterate rural communities, then the formal rules simply had to be disregarded or broken. Pre-colonial political institutions (chieftaincies), in this instance very effectively destroyed by the French, could not be reconstituted to cope with this problem of political communication. So new categories of African intermediaries emerged from the subject masses and established a political network outside the formal government apparatus, but indispensable to it. To break the rules therefore became a well-entrenched habit, long before Senegal's independence, and today these 'violations' are so firmly established and informally codified as to have become virtually institutions in their own right (or wrong).

While introducing a bureaucratic system of government, always more or less unviable but still in place today, the colonial authorities also of course brought about very rapid changes in the social and economic spheres. And for the Wolof at least, the people in Senegal most affected by these changes (urbanisation, the peanut economy, etc.), this meant a constant re-definition of the bases of social action. If one may assume (and I think one may) that most Wolof, most of the time, acted within the limits of their opportunities to maximise their own wealth and power, then this also implied initially a political upheaval as new chances became available. Later, as certain limits to opportunity became apparent, political action could be more clearly codified. But if insiders proceeded with due hesitation and experiment to test the political scope allowed to them by a changing social environment, outsiders may properly also show some hesitation in describing the procedures involved. Many of the best-established categories of political sociology, widely used by authorities on similar colonial and post-colonial situations, offer only a dubious guidance to the observer of Wolof politics over this whole period (1850–1973).

These familiar categories (whether for example of Weberian or Marxian derivation) have indeed been employed in various contexts in the above essays, but it is recognised that a certain revisionism is required if the labels are not to become instruments of distortion rather than clarification. This is very obviously the case for the category of traditional social action. Many Wolof did of course continue to act as they believed their forbears to have done, doubtless without pondering unduly over the principles involved. But in the historical period under consideration, it was never quite a simple matter to look to 'what has always existed' for guidance. Within Wolof society there were in fact two important competing traditions (semi-pagan and Muslim) which furthermore had been at odds for several centuries prior to French conquest. After the conquest, with the drastic social re-ordering of colonial rule, 'tradition' could still be the basis of a (conservative) ideological stance, but it could not be acted out consistently in social or political life.

For such circumstances of (in effect) revolutionary social upheaval, Weber might of course have predicted the emergence of new social movements of his charismatic type. And some Wolof did act true to form, at least in the Mouride brotherhood. But even at the very outset, true charismatic exuberance and the hysterical adulation of an exemplary leader were mingled with a variety of worldly ambitions and a marked (if disguised) reluctance to follow the heroic example. So Wolof charisma emerges as a force in the material as well as the ideal world: for the devotees, charisma is identified with the money and power in the hands of the bearers of the divine gift. And charismatic community never precluded individual strife and self-promotion.

Other categories of collective social and political action might also be mentioned, as requiring some re-definition in the Wolof context. The Marxian category of class is an obvious example: Marxian Africanists in general talk more readily of the process of 'class formation' than of true social classes in Africa's post-colonial states.[1] For the Wolof and for Senegal, one might add that there is nothing ineluctable even in the process. The opposed interests of urban government officials and rural producers have yet to be clearly organised and expressed in political terms, and in the last essay here we have noted important reservations as to the likely future emergence of conflict along these lines. Inequalities of wealth and power within rural Wolof society seem even less likely to find corporate political expression.

Even the apparently less contentious, descriptive social categories of tribe and Sufi brotherhood have their own problems of political definition. The Wolof have their own language and culture, but they seem quite willing to share them with other Senegalese 'tribes'. At the same time internal divisions within Wolof society seem for the moment to preclude their corporate tribal political action. Perhaps indeed a process of 'tribe formation' is at work among other Senegalese linguistic and cultural groups, such as has indeed been discerned elsewhere in Africa,[2] but for the present one can only say that it is less than apparent. Politics in many other African states may revolve around tribal issues: not so at least in Senegal. For the Wolof, one may indeed wonder in what sense they are a tribe at all – certainly a true Wolof tribalist would see important problems ahead in raising the level of corporate political consciousness.

Political solidarity within Senegal's Muslim brotherhoods is a similarly dubious matter. The French colonisers, in choosing the label 'brotherhood' (*confrérie*) for the Sufi *tariqa*, and in acting on the assumption that these were corporate organisational entities, undoubtedly contributed to a certain confusion here. The loosely co-ordinated structure of the pre-colonial *tariqa* might better have been labelled that of a religious 'order' (as indeed is prevalent English-language practice). But French interest in the subject was administrative rather than scholarly, and French policy was to make the brotherhood a viable intermediary agency of government: instructions once received from French authority would be passed down the local religious hierarchy. To a limited degree the French were in a position to make a political reality of their initially misguided judgment, most notably so in the Mouride case. But even in this case, and more clearly in the case of Senegal's other Muslim 'brotherhoods', the notion of corporate allegiance to a strict hierarchy of spiritual leaders remained little more than a French bureaucrat's dream.

In examining political action among the Wolof, then, these various established categories of corporate political action (traditional, charismatic, class-based, tribal, Muslim segmentary) are of no more than partial assistance, and in some instances may even be a hindrance to the observer. Not that sociologically defined groups are irrelevant to Wolof political life: in this instance at least, one need not be driven to the Hobbesian conclusions of one observer of African politics, the vision of a 'war of all against all'.[3] Wolof (and Senegalese) politics is not to be understood merely as a struggle of isolated individuals, senseless in any other terms than those of each individual's drive to better his own material position at the expense of others. A concentration on individual self-interest may nonetheless serve as a useful starting point in developing a sociological understanding of Senegalese political strife. Real solidarities do exist, though they may vary from situation to situation, and though they may not correspond very closely to many familiar sociological categories. The crucial political categories are those already outlined in the last of these essays, those of the network of 'clan' alliances which are so characteristic of Senegalese political life. In other words, one returns to a phenomenology of the politics of corruption: just how, precisely, are the Senegalese 'corrupt'?

There is no single pat answer to such a question. Corruption may be defined in general terms as the breach of institutional rules for private material gain, usually working to the advantage of a privileged elite – a kleptocracy, in one telling neologism.[4] But in the Senegalese context at least, many complicating factors intervene to cloud this transparent simplicity. Material gain can assume different forms, from straightforward cash misappropriation to more complex advantages in terms of status hegemony or political power. And the gain is never, or at least very rarely, an exclusively private matter. The political actors, even in a kleptocracy, need trustworthy friends if they are to get ahead. And even the most self-seeking members of the governing elite may find it useful to dispense favours to those below them as well as to elite cronies. All of this proceeds in violation of institutional regulations, but it should be obvious that the umbrella term 'corruption' can cover a very wide range of empirical possibilities.

The very use of the word, corruption, itself suggests a note of moral indignation more clearly than it does an analytical perspective. And in Senegal at least, it is part of the language of political actors: to an outside observer it may be confusing, and also somewhat disarming, to realise that the most devious of Senegalese politicians are among the most vehement in their denunciations of the prevalence of corruption. The politician of course does not denounce himself, but he does denounce his own kind. This fact in itself may impose a certain dubious reticence on the outsider before stating his own moral preferences. And any reasonably close observation of local political activity does reveal the moral dimension in many formally illicit arrangements – whether between equals in a political faction, or between unequals in a patron-client relation. Senegalese clan morality has already been portrayed as a more or less necessary complement to the fragile convergence of individual material interest.

For an outside evaluation of the Senegalese political style, one may begin by remembering the victims, those who fall outside the moral boundaries surrounding political or economic transactions. The Senegalese writer Ousmane Sembène, in his short story and film 'The Money Order' (*Le Mandat*) offers a bitter and relevant parable. An elderly, simple citizen receives a money order for some fifty pounds from his nephew, a Paris street-cleaner. His ultimately futile efforts to cash the order lead him helpless into the maze of Dakar bureaucracy, while he is hoodwinked and swindled by cynical functionaries, by usurer-traders, then last, most bitterly and most comprehensively, by his own family. The helpless innocent is of course a useful focus to such a moral tale, and the tale though very simple is also powerful (as well as funny). Cynical and parasitic elite as against trusting shantytown victim, it is not difficult to read the moral and the political lesson. The best of Africa's recent imaginative literature (by Chinua Achebe and A. K. Armah for example) revolves around similar themes, the portrait of societies in the course of moral disintegration.[5]

To conclude these essays one must I think recognise the force of this 'imaginative' vision, but one must also understand that 'the elite' and 'the mass' are no more than (further) convenient labels to cover a diverse social reality. From among the mass, one may find a higher proportion of true innocents in fiction than in real social life. The victims are not unaware of the political games which go on around them, often at their expense: they take the trouble to try to learn the rules, and to use them (so far as possible) to their own advantage. The elite predators may be distinguished into given categories, each with a distinct style of operation. Four principal categories, four styles of more or less corrupt activity, will be briefly reviewed here: the bureaucrat, the party politician, the private trader, and the saint. The four styles, once they have been separately presented and summarily explained, can then be seen as aspects of a larger style.

The Senegalese state official may properly be regarded as a near-perfect realisation of Andreski's ideal-typical notion of the kleptocrat. Public servants not merely account for over half the national budget in official salaries, they use their control of administrative and marketing institutions to make further illicit profits on a scale roughly proportional to each individual's standing within the official hierarchy. The local bureaucrat, whose style of life is still modelled on that of his French predecessors, finds that he cannot hope to attain such relative luxury without systematically breaking the rules of his organisation. The differential exercise of administrative power can be a means to draw cash subsidies from the bureaucrat's wealthier clients, and protection money from the politically weak (e.g. the local Lebanese). Private commerce can be conducted under the formal auspices and protection of state authority, and (at its simplest) cash can just be stolen from the till. In these procedures certain limited bases of commercial and political solidarity do emerge: with party politicians who can (at a price) provide security from the harassment of official investigation, with traders who can provide remunerative outlets for administrative funds, and of course with family members (not many) who help to consume the funds. These are solidarities of the privileged, of an elite which shows little concern for patronage expenditures to the subject masses.

The bureaucrat's crucial advantages are his education and specialised training, which make his activities mysterious and unintelligible to many of the subjects, as well as his institutional position as an officer of the state. Though systematically breaking his own supposed rules, he can in fact manipulate the rules to hoodwink quite a proportion of the people some of the time. The people may not have the means to understand just *how* they are being swindled, but it must be said that they do (at least among the Wolof) realise that they *are* swindled. The apparatus of Senegalese officialdom is locally seen at least in broad outline as a parasitic body, and it certainly does seem to provide small proportional return for the legal and illegal salaries of its sixty thousand employees.

The party politician, even in the Senegalese single-party state, must regard his position as dependent to some degree on popular support (or at the very least, a plausible appearance of popular support). Officials of the *Union Progressiste Sénégalaise* are at least in principle chosen by election from below, and must always in fact bear their supporters in mind. To neglect the constituency, at any level in the party hierarchy, is to risk losing one's job. Thus the party officer, though involved in many elite intrigues for private financial gain (corruption), is also concerned to redistribute some of the proceeds especially to the more influential of his supporters. The bureaucrat, who has no constituency but only a temporary area of jurisdiction, need only be concerned with the good opinion of his superiors (and that too can be bought): the proceeds of his malversation ultimately find their way to Dakar. The party official is valued by his superiors largely for the support which he is deemed to command in his constituency (a term which may be understood in broad sociological terms rather than a legal and restrictive sense). To command that support, it is well understood that he must be shown to have secured favourable government consideration for his constituents. This is the corruption of machine politics, in which the party man may be seen as counterpose to the bureaucrat you can't swindle all the people all the time, not even country people.

The private trader may seem a dubious candidate for analysis in this perspective of corruption. He is after all by profession dedicated to the pursuit of private gain, and thus apparently cannot violate his own commercial norms in the maximisation of profits. From the rural Wolof he buys peanuts, to them he lends money and sells a range of (largely imported) commodities. But money-lending and peanut-buying are each conducted outside the boundaries of Senegalese law, which means that the goal of profit-maximisation can only be achieved with the help of political protection. Bureaucrats and party officials receive their cut, and the successful trader is in fact one who is as skilful in political intrigue as in strictly commercial transactions. He may not break his own rules, but his success depends on breaking the rules of others. His 'clientele' is not to be understood as a constituency of candidates for patronage redistribution, rather as those with whom he does business (buys and sells) and who are dependent usually because they owe him money. He is from the peasant's standpoint naturally enough often a detested figure, however indispensable his services on occasion may be. From the outside he appears above all as the ally of the state bureaucracy in a whole range of corrupt manipulations – corruption of and for the elite. The peasants indeed are necessarily and permanently the losers in their encounters with bureaucratic/commercial graft of this type.

The saint does of course take his part in the politics of the elite, he does further his political and commercial ends by alliances with given bureaucrats, traders and party representatives. But he is to be distinguished from these allies by the nature of his relations with his own disciples. Alone among the privileged in this respect, he has his roots in peasant society: the saint's relation to his disciples, including the differential exchange of goods and services, has a real, locally recognised moral sanction – most simply, paradise. The saint, like the trader, may participate in violating the supposed norms of others at an elite level. In dealing with his own peasant disciples, however, he must take his own divinely-sanctioned principles more seriously. These principles are shared by the disciples, who indeed have done much to develop their implications in the material world. The client is far from helpless before his holy patron, indeed he expects his saint to act as his protector in dealing with the other superordinate agents of the Senegalese state. It is the very effectiveness of the saintly intermediary in this respect which makes the agencies of state authority acceptable to the Muslim peasant. The charismatic community also depends for its survival on the material services which accompany the divine gift, in other words on the ways in which the saintly variant of elite corruption can be shown to have brought some real benefits to the peasant masses.

The Wolof peasants, though they are in many respects and to varying degrees the victims of the ruling elite, cannot thus be seen as inert objects of exploitation from above. Through the saints, and to a lesser extent through local party representatives, peasants can assert their own particular claims. These claims (for the preferential allocation of government services) can often only be satisfied by procedures in violation of formal institutional arrangements. So corruption does not work solely to the advantage of the already privileged: indeed the total eradication of corruption from the Senegalese state (admittedly a remote eventuality) might well leave the peasants altogether defenceless before a technically qualified bureaucracy.

Having sketched some of the political procedures in Senegal which may be labelled as 'corrupt' it remains to answer the final question – why are the Senegalese so adept in the politics of corruption? A part of the answer has already been suggested, in the peculiarly effective synthesis of a rural political tradition (that of the Muslim orders or brotherhoods) with a long-established urban one (that of the commune factions). The saints, with their solid basis in rural society and their knowledge of the ways of the urban elite, act both to translate the city's demands and to cushion their peasant disciples from the full impact of bureaucratic state or market economy – pretending to be the policemen of the elite in such a manner that the disciples will regard them as the best (if not for them the only) way to get around the urban elite's version of the law. Money, literacy, a habit of political intrigue perfected under colonial rule, all contribute to the saints' success in acting out their ambiguous role. And it all works well enough at least so far as the (rural) Wolof are concerned. If the Wolof peasants are the economic backbone of the Senegalese state, the saints help to ensure that the state (licitly and otherwise) returns at least a sufficient proportion to preclude anything like a Wolof peasant insurrection.

The urban-based political elite (bureaucrats, traders, party representatives) has of course developed its own internal cohesion through the various illicit arrangements already enumerated – those covered by the local term, clan politics. It is proper to give a degree of credit, finally, to the French for having provided some of the basis in political education for the practise of this style of politics. The Senegalese have indeed drawn their own conclusions and adapted their lessons to local conditions, but it is I think important that many of the leading Senegalese politicians (Blaise Diagne, Lamine Guèye, Léopold Senghor) learned their skills originally in the sophisticated instability of Paris under the Third and Fourth Republics. A certain political diffusion operated from Paris to the electoral manipulations of the Senegalese communes, municipalities and elective assemblies. Training in French techniques of parliamentary and other political intrigue was certainly no corruption of innocents, and some of the pupils became adroit enough to teach a few lessons to their French masters. The Senegalese through French experience were exposed to a political tradition of relevance to their own problems: the local political elite did not learn their craft from texts or sermons on The Westminster Model, nor from equally arid authorities of European Socialism. They learned by experience, in the tough and devious bargaining of Gauloise-filled rooms in Paris. And after Senegal's independence they did not have to proceed by haphazard trial and error to explore the application of these lessons to local conditions. Through the long colonial experience of electoral politics in the coastal communes, later through the territorial assembly, they had adapted a knowledge of French political practise first to Senegalese urban conditions, then to the countryside.

The style of politics which has emerged from this experience, with its little touch of Gallic flair as well as a purely Senegalese exuberance, cannot perhaps in conscience be proposed as a model for other African states to imitate. There will not, in the first place, be another chance for Africans to participate in the political haggling and bartering of French (or of course British) parliaments. There are also few (if any) African states with rural political institutions of the proven flexibility and durability of Senegal's Muslim brotherhoods: and without such institutions, political ties between urban elite and rural mass are often fragile indeed. Despite these obvious reservations, there is at the very least a body of political experience here of equally obvious relevance to problems in the organisation of post-colonial states elsewhere. But for Senegal itself, one must fear for the future viability of the local political style in the light of the country's continuing economic stagnation. Beyond the immediate danger to the lives of many rural citizens, there looms an eventual threat to the whole of established social and political organisation. The prognosis for a spoils system cannot be good when the means of corruption become exhausted.

NOTES

1 For some elaborations of a Marxian schema, see G. Arrighi and J. S. Saul, *Essays on the Political Economy of Africa*, New York: Monthly Review Press, 1973; also S. Amin, *L'Afrique de l'Ouest Bloquée*, Paris: Eds. de Minuit, 1971 (paperback translation *Neo-Colonialism in West Africa*, Penguin, 1973); R. First, *The Barrel of a Gun*, London: Allen Lane, 1970.

2 Notably by modern social anthropologists, working in a variety of African states (Nigeria, Kenya, Zambia and others). The points emphasised here being that modern communications possibilities and organisational forms have given new cohesion to tribal categories – especially in the towns. An intelligent discussion of the problem by a political scientist can be found in Crawford Young, *Politics in the Congo*, Princeton: Princeton University Press, 1965 (Chapter 11 on 'Ethnicity', pp. 239–78).
See also, in this context, M. G. Smith's interesting use of the concept of 'pluralism'. L. Kuper and M. G. Smith (eds.), *Pluralism in Africa*, Berkeley and Los Angeles: University of California Press, 1969.

3 S. Andreski, *The African Predicament*, London: Michael Joseph, 1968, pp. 72, 164.

4 Andreski, pp. 92–109.

5 See especially these two novels: Chinua Achebe, *A Man of the People*, London: Heinemann, 1966; Ayi Kwei Armah, *The Beautyful Ones are Not Yet Born*, Boston: Houghton Mifflin, 1968. Ousmane Sembène's tale was first published in French as a short story, and has since been made a ninety-minute film (in Wolof, French sub-titles) directed by the author. Those unable to see the film may read the story in his *Vehi-Ciosane ou Blanc-Genèse Suivi du Mandat*, Paris: Présence Africaine, 1966.

Reference bibliography

ARCHIVES

Archives Nationales, Section Outre-Mer, Paris (A.N.S.O.M.).
Archives de la République du Sénégal, Dakar (A.R.S.D.).

NEWSPAPERS AND PERIODICALS

(a) SENEGALESE

L'Action Sénégalaise (St Louis, 1932–4, weekly).
L'A.O.F. (Dakar, 1912–58, irregular).
Condition Humaine (Dakar, 1948–56, irregular).
Dakar-Matin (Dakar, 1960–, daily).
L'Opposition (Dakar, 1932, two numbers only).
L'Ouest Africain Français (Dakar, 1925–6, weekly).
Le Périscope Africain (Dakar, 1931–2, 1936, weekly).

(b) OTHER

Bulletin de la Congrégation du Saint-Esprit (Paris, biennial, 1903–4).
Le Monde (Paris, daily).
West Africa (London, weekly).

OFFICIAL

Afrique Occidentale Française, Haut Commisariat, Service de la Statistique Générale, *Commune Mixte de Thiès: Recensement de 1953*. Dakar: n.d.
Recensement Démographique de Dakar (1955) Paris, 1958.

Reference bibliography

Afrique Occidentale Française, Territoire du Sénégal, *Aménagement de l'Economie Agricole et Rurale du Sénégal*, Dakar, 1952.
Rapport sur L'Activité des Services, Dakar, 1954.
Documentation Française, La, *Notes et Etudes Documentaires*, No. 2508, Paris, 1959.
Sénégal, République du, *Bulletin Economique et Statistique*, Dakar, periodical. *Situation Economique et Statistique*, Dakar, annual.
Journal Officiel, Numero Spécial, 30 Mai 1960.
Rapport Général sur les Perspectives de Développement du Sénégal, Dakar: CINAM, 1960.
Rapport de Synthèse, Dakar: CINAM, 1964.
'Note sur la Situation Agricole du Sénégal', Dakar: Conseil Economique et Social, 1966, Annexe No. 31.
United States Army, *Area Handbook for Senegal*, Washington D.C., 1963.

BOOKS, ARTICLES AND UNPUBLISHED DOCUMENTS

Achebe, C. *A Man of the People*, London: Heinemann, 1966.
Ames, D. W. 'Belief in "Witches" among the rural Wolof of the Gambia' in *Africa*, Vol. XXIX, No. 3, 1959.
'The Economic Base of Wolof Polygyny' in *South-Western Journal of Anthropology*, Vol. XI, No. 4, 1955.
'The Selection of Mates, Courtship and Marriage among the Wolof' in *Bulletin de L'Institut Français D'Afrique Noire*, Vol. XVIII, Ser. B, Nos. 1–2, 1956.
'Wolof Cooperative Work Groups' in W. R. Bascom and M. J. Herskovits (eds.), *Continuity and Change in African Cultures*, Chicago: University of Chicago Press, 1959.
Amin, S. *L'Afrique de l'Ouest Bloquée*, Paris: Eds. de Minuit, 1971, now available in translation as *Neo-Colonialism in West Africa*, Harmondsworth: Penguin African Library, 1973.
Andreski, S. *The African Predicament*, London: Michael Joseph, 1968.
Armah, A. K. *The Beautyful Ones are Not Yet Born*, Boston: Houghton Mifflin, 1968.
Arnaud, R. *L'Islam et la Politique Musulmane Française en Afrique Occidentale Française*, Paris: Afrique Française, 1912.
Précis de Politique Musulmane, Alger: Jourdain, 1906.

Arrighi, G. and J. S. Saul. *Essays on the Political Economy of Africa*, New York: Monthly Review Press, 1973.

Bailey, F. G. *Stratagems and Spoils*, Oxford: Blackwell, 1969.

Bedu, T. *Cours de Droit: Legislation Foncière*, Bambey Sénégal: Ecole Nationale des Cadres Ruraux, 1964 (unpublished).

Behrman, L. C. *Muslim Brotherhoods and Politics in Senegal*, Cambridge Mass.: Harvard University Press, 1970.

Betts, R. *Assimilation and Association in French Colonial Theory, 1890–1914*, New York: Columbia University Press, 1961.

Bouchaud, F. *L'Eglise en Afrique Noire*, Paris: La Palatine, 1958.

Brochier, J. *La Diffusion du Progrès Technique en Milieu Rural Sénégalais*, Dakar: Ecole Nationale d'Economie Appliquée, 1966.

Brosselard, C. *Rapport sur la Situation de la Vallée du Sénégal en 1886*, Lille: Danel, 1888.

Buell, R. L. *The Native Problem in Africa*, London: Cass, 1965 – first published 1928.

Camboulives, M. *L'Organisation Co-opérative au Sénégal*, Paris: Eds. Pedone, 1967.

Centre de Hautes Etudes Administratives sur l'Afrique et l'Asie Modernes (ed.). *Notes et Etudes sur l'Islam en Afrique Noire*, Paris: Peyronnet, 1962.

Copans, J. *et al. Maintenance Sociale et Changement Economique au Sénégal*, Vol. I, *Doctrine Economique et Pratique du Travail chez les Mourides*, Paris: O.R.S.T.O.M., 1972.

Copans, J. 'Stratification Sociale et Organisation du Travail Agricole dans les Villages Wolof Mourides du Sénégal', Paris, Ecole Pratique des Hautes Etudes, *Thèse de 3e cycle*, 1973 (unpublished).

Cottingham, C. 'Clan Politics and Rural Modernisation', Ph.D. Thesis, University of California Berkeley, 1969 (unpublished).

'Political Consolidation and Centre-Local Relations in Senegal', in *The Canadian Journal of African Studies*, Vol. 4, No. 1, Winter 1970.

Cruise O'Brien, D. *The Mourides of Senegal*, Oxford: Clarendon Press, 1971.

'Towards an Islamic Policy in French West Africa, 1854–1914', in *Journal of African History*, Vol. VIII, No. 2, 1967.

'Political Opposition in Senegal', in *Government and Opposition*, Vol. 2, No. 4, July–October 1967.

'Le talibé mouride', in *Cahiers d'Etudes Africaines* (C.E.A.), No. 35,

1969 and *C.E.A.*, No. 40, 1970.
'The Saint and the Squire', in C. Allen and W. Johnson (eds.), *African Perspectives*, Cambridge: Cambridge University Press, 1970.
Cruise O'Brien, Rita. *White Society in Black Africa. The French of Senegal*, London: Faber, 1972.
'Colonialism to Cooperation? French Technical Assistance in Senegal', in *The Journal of Development Studies*, Vol. 8, No. 1, October 1971.
Decraene, P. 'Le Sénégal, dix ans après l'Indépendance', *Le Monde* 20–3 August 1970.
Delcourt, A. *La France et les Etablissements Français au Sénégal (1713–1764)*, Dakar: I.F.A.N., 1952.
Depont, O. and Coppolani, X. *Les Confréries Religieuses Musulmanes*, Alger: Jourdain, 1897.
Des Isles, P. 'Contribution à l'Etude du Mouridisme', St Louis (Senegal): 1948 (unpublished).
Dore, R. P. 'Traditional Communities and Modern Cooperatives', in P. Worsley (ed.), *Two Blades of Grass*, Manchester: Manchester University Press, 1971.
Dumont, F. 'Essai sur la Pensée Religieuse d'Amadou Bamba', *Thèse de Doctorat*, Université de Dakar, 1968 (unpublished).
Dumont, R. *L'Afrique Noire est mal Partie*, Paris: Seuil, 1962.
First, R. *The Barrel of a Gun*, London: Allen Lane, 1970.
Gamble, D. *The Wolof of Senegambia*, London: International African Institute, 1957.
Ganier, G. 'Lat Dyor et le Chemin de Fer de l'Arachide', *Bulletin de l'I.F.A.N.* Vol. XXVII, 1965.
Geertz, C. *Islam Observed*, New Haven and London: Yale University Press, 1968.
Gellar, S. 'The Politics of Development in Senegal', Ph.D. Thesis in Politics, Columbia University, 1967 (unpublished).
Guèye, M. 'L'Affaire Chautemps (Avril 1904) et la suppression de l'esclavage de case au Sénégal', in *Bulletin de l'I.F.A.N.*, Vol. XXVII, Série B, Nos. 3–4, 1965.
Guiraud, X. *L'Arachide Sénégalaise*, Paris: Librarie Technique et Economique, 1937.
Hardy, G. *La Mise en Valeur du Sénégal de 1817 à 1854*, Paris: Larose, 1921.
I.R.F.E.D., 'Le Sénégal en Marche', *Les Cahiers Africains*, No. 5, 1962.
Johnson, G.W. *The Emergence of Black Politics in Senegal*. Stanford:

Stanford University Press, 1971.

Kilson, M. *Political Change in a West African State*, Cambridge, Mass.: Harvard University Press, 1966.

Klein, M. *Islam and Imperialism in Senegal, Sine-Saloum 1847–1914*, Edinburgh: Edinburgh University Press, 1968.

'Slavery, the Slave Trade, and Legitimate Commerce in Late Nineteenth Century Africa', in *Etudes d'Histoire Africaine*, Vol. II, 1971.

'Revolution and Social Change in Nineteenth Century Senegambia', Toronto, n.d. (unpublished).

Kuper, L. and M. G. Smith (eds.). *Pluralism in Africa*, Berkeley and Los Angeles: University of California Press, 1969.

Landé, C. H. *Leaders, Factions, and Parties: the Structure of Philippine Politics*, Yale University, Southeast Asia Monographs, 1966.

Landsberger, H. A. 'Social and Political Preconditions for Co-operatives among poor farmers in the United States South', in P. Worsley (ed.), *Two Blades of Grass . . .*

Le Chatelier, A. *L'Islam dans L'Afrique Occidentale*, Paris: Steinheil, 1899

Leiris, M. *L'Afrique Fantôme*, Paris: Gallimard, 1934.

Lemarchand, R. and K. Legg. 'Political Clientelism and Development', in *Comparative Politics*, Vol. 4, No. 2. 1972.

Ly, A. *L'Etat et la Production Paysanne*, Paris: Présence Africaine, 1958.

Mannheim, K. *Ideology and Utopia* (Gerth and Shils trans.), New York: Harcourt Brace, 1964 (first published 1936).

Marty, P. *Les Mourides d'Amadou Bamba,* Paris: Leroux, 1913.

Etudes sur l'Islam au Sénégal, Paris: Leroux, 1917.

Marx, K. 'The Eighteenth Brumaire of Louis Bonaparte', in Marx and Engels, *Selected Works*, London: Lawrence and Wishart, 1962, Vol. I.

Meillassoux, C. (ed.). *The Development of Indigenous Trade and Markets in West Africa*, London: Oxford University Press, 1971.

Mergane, M. 'Rapport sur les Co-opératives dans l'Arrondissement de Ndame', Dakar: Ecole Nationale d'Economie Appliquée, 1965 (unpublished thesis).

Mollien, G. T. *L'Afrique Occidentale en 1818*, Paris: Calmann-Lévy, 1967 (first published in 1820).

Monteil, V. *Esquisses Sénégalaises*, Dakar: Institut Fondamental d'Afrique Noire (I.F.A.N.), 1966.

'Une Confrérie Musulmane: les Mourides du Sénégal', in *Archives de Sociologie des Religions*, No. 14, 1962.

Moore, B. Jr. *Social Origins of Dictatorship and Democracy. Lord and Peasant in the Making of the Modern World*, Boston: Beacon Press, 1967.

Ndiaye, A. 'L'Assistance aux Co-opératives, leur Développement', in *Développement et Civilisations* (special number), 1962.

Nekkach, L. 'Le Mouridisme Depuis 1912', St Louis-Sénégal, unpublished, 1952.

Pélissier, P. *Les Paysans du Sénégal. Les Civilisations Agraires du Cayor à la Casamance*, St Yrieix: Imp. Fabrègue, 1966.

Quellien, A. *La Politique Musulmane en Afrique Occidentale Française*, Paris: Larose, 1910.

Quesnot, F. 'L'Evolution du Tidjanisme Sénégalais, depuis 1922', Paris: *Centre de Hautes Etudes Administratives sur l'Afrique et l'Asie Modernes*, *Mémoire*, No. 2865, 1958 (unpublished).

Reverdy, J. C. *Une Société Rurale au Sénégal: les Structures Foncières, Familiales, et Villageoises des Serer*, Aix-en-Provence, Centre Africain des Sciences Humaines Appliquées, 1968.

Riggs, F. *Administration in Developing Countries,* Boston: Houghton Mifflin, 1964.

Robinson, K.E. 'The *Sociétés de Prévoyance* in French West Africa', in *Journal of African Administration*, Vol. II, 1950.

'Senegal', in Robinson and W. J. M. Mackenzie (eds.). *Five Elections in Africa*, Oxford: Clarendon Press, 1960.

Rocheteau, G. *Système Mouride et Rapports Sociaux Traditionnels,* Dakar: O.R.S.T.O.M. 1969 (unpublished).

'Samb', A. M. *Cadoir Demb*, Dakar: Imprimerie Diop, 1964.

Sembène, O. *Vehi-Ciosane ou Blanc-Genèse Suivi du Mandat*, Paris: Présence Africaine, 1966.

Silla, O. 'Les Castes dans la Société Ouolof', *Mémoire*, Ecole Pratique des Hautes Etudes (Paris). 1965 (unpublished).

Snyder, G. *One-Party Government in Mali*, New Haven: Yale University Press, 1965.

Suret-Canale, J. 'La Fin de la Chefferie en Guinée', in *Journal of African History*, Vol. VII, No. 3, 1966.

Sy, C. T. *La Confrérie Sénégalaise des Mourides*, Paris: Présence Africaine, 1969.

Thibaud, P. 'Dia, Senghor, et le Socialisme Africain', in *Esprit*, No. 9, Sept. 1963.

Thomas, L. V. *Les Diola*, Dakar: Institut Français de l'Afrique Noire, 1958.

Trimingham, J.S. *Islam in West Africa*, Oxford: Clarendon Press, 1959.

A History of Islam in West Africa, Oxford: Clarendon Press, 1962.

Verrière, L. 'La Population du Sénégal' *Thèse de Doctorat*, Faculté de Droit et Sciences Economiques, Université de Dakar, 1965 (unpublished).

Wade, A. 'La Doctrine Economique du Mouridisme', Dakar, 1966 (unpublished).

Weber, M. (H. Gerth and C. Wright Mills [ed. and trans.]), *From Max Weber*, London and New York: Oxford University Press, 1946.

Weiner, M. (ed.). *Modernization*, New York: Basic Books, 1967.

Worsley, P. *The Trumpet Shall Sound*, London: Paladin Edition, 1970 (first published 1957).

(ed.) *Two Blades of Grass*. Manchester: Manchester University Press, 1971.

Young, C. *Politics in the Congo*, Princeton: Princeton University Press, 1965.

Yung, J.M. 'Aperçus sur le Système Co-operatif Sénégalais', Dakar: S.A.T.E.C. 1966 (unpublished).

Zolberg, A. *Creating Political Order*, Chicago: Rand McNally, 1966, pp. 73–7.

Zuccarelli, F. *Un Parti Politique Africain*, Paris: Pichon et Durand-Auzias, 1970.

Index

Soc
DT
549.42
C77